June '86

The Christian Woman's

The
Christian Woman's
Resource Book

Melba Graf Burroughs

THE WESTMINSTER PRESS
Philadelphia

ACKNOWLEDGMENTS
The Lockman Foundation, for Scripture quotations from the *Amplified New Testament.* Copyright © The Lockman Foundation 1954, 1958.

National Council of the Churches of Christ in the U.S.A., for verses from the Revised Standard Version of the Bible copyrighted 1946, 1952, © 1971, 1973 by the Division of Christian Education of the National Council of the Churches of Christ in the U.S.A.

Tyndale House Publishers, for verses from *The Living Bible,* copyright 1971 by Tyndale House Publishers, Wheaton, Ill.

Zondervan Bible Publishers, for Scripture taken from the *Amplified Bible, Old Testament,* Copyright © 1962, 1964 by Zondervan Publishing House, and from the *Holy Bible: New International Version,* Copyright © 1978 by the New York International Bible Society.

Book Design by Alice Derr

First edition

Bridgebooks
Published by The Westminster Press®
Philadelphia, Pennsylvania

PRINTED IN THE UNITED STATES OF AMERICA
9 8 7 6 5 4 3 2 1

Library of Congress Cataloging in Publication Data

Burroughs, Melba Graf, 1928–
   The Christian woman's resource book.

   "Bridgebooks."
   1. Women—Religious life. I. Title.
BV4527.B87 1984   248.8'43   83-26063
ISBN 0-664-26008-X (pbk.)

TO
EDWARD, my love,
and
DWIGHT and DEBBIE BURROUGHS
RENÉE and BILL SNIDER
Who came from that love

Contents

Preface

Today, as Christian women, we find that there are more pressures, tugs, and demands on us than ever before.

We are expected to be a caring daughter to our parents, a perfect homemaker, a loving wife to our husband, a good mother to our children. And some of us even have an added title—that special grandmother! And if we work outside our home—as many of us do—we must also be the efficient and hardworking employer or employee.

Then there are the demands and obligations to our church, our community, our school, and our friends and neighbors.

It seems we wear so many hats that we often feel that the person we really are—the real *I* inside us—gets lost, or splits and breaks into a thousand pieces.

Yet, regardless of the circumstances about us, we, as Christian women, are most blessed among women, for we have a bounty of spiritual resources to draw from for help in any situation that life presents to us. We have the advantage of spiritual assistance in everything from dealing with a personal identity crisis and establishing better relationships to fulfilling our highest potential or facing any challenge that comes our way.

But often, even though we are Christians, we do not know we have all these spiritual resources. Or if we do know, somehow we aren't able to make them work in our lives.

Recently a friend told me: "I know about the good news of the gospel and I am a believer. I go to church, read my Bible, and pray."

Then she added: "But I am also miserable, afraid, and feel inadequate to meet life's challenges. The constant crises of life seem to overwhelm me continually. I feel torn apart."

I knew what she meant. Sometime ago I felt the same way. I knew Christian principles and could quote Scripture for every occasion. But I didn't know how to apply the Christian resources to my needs—right now, this moment—where I was hurting.

And when I learned how, it made all the difference in my life.

In this book, I will explore not only the needs of Christian women in today's fast-paced world but also how we can have the help of special Christian spiritual resources in our lives.

After you have read this book and applied these Christian principles to your needs, this statement made by Jesus will not be just words but will become a reality in every area of your life.

I came that they may have and enjoy life, and have it in abundance—to the full, till it overflows. (John 10:10, AMP)

M.G.B.

Maplelot
Dallas

Introduction to the Banquet Table

Women's needs are many.

But God's resources are greater.

Through Christian principles we can find an answer for every challenge we might face. There is a healing balm for every disappointment, disillusionment, and sorrow. And we can find inspiration, guidance, and strength, because God's resources show us how we, as women, can reach our highest potential.

The resources we are talking about are not mystical, vague, or so esoteric that we cannot apply them to our life in today's world. On the contrary, God's principles and provisions are so practical, workable, and evidential that, when properly understood, they can lift up and make better every area of our life.

Understanding God's resources opens up the shutters of our life and lets the sunlight in. We see blue skies, and even on cloudy days there is a rainbow breaking through.

Christian resources, no matter how helpful and life-changing, can work only if we put them to work, for those are the rules of the principles involved. We must understand and utilize the resources while we align ourselves with our Source. God warned his people that they would perish for lack of knowledge (Hos. 4:6). So the more we know and understand and apply concerning God's provisions, the better our life can be.

Too often we find ourselves acting like an elderly school-teacher named Hattie, who saved for many years to go on a cruise. Finally she had enough money for the cruise ticket but very little money left for food. Hattie was used to scrimping and forgoing luxuries, so she brought enough peanut butter and crackers, cheese and canned beans to last until the last night of the cruise. Then she would splurge and spend the little money she had on a fine meal.

Hattie enjoyed the cruise immensely, but mealtimes were difficult. She would march around the huge banquet tables and view the rich foods—the steamship rounds of roast beef, the fat browned turkeys, and the ducklings with orange sauce. She saw the huge piles of boiled shrimp and of lobster tails, and the silver bowls of caviar. Then there were rows and rows of dishes of colorful vegetables, baskets of exotic fruits, and enough desserts—cakes, pies, fancy ices—to make her mouth water.

But all Hattie could do was look and then go back to her stateroom and eat the peanut butter and crackers.

Finally the last night of the cruise arrived. Hattie dressed in her finest clothes and went to the dining room to eat with the rest of the passengers. The meal was everything she had dreamed it would be.

The time came to pay. Hattie called the waiter over to ask him for the check.

"Madam," he said gently. "There is no charge. Didn't you know that your meals were included when you bought your ticket?"

Too often we, as Christian women, find ourselves in Hattie's position. We have a banquet table of Christian resources spread before us. They belong to us as believers. But we don't realize the bounty is ours, so we don't take advantage of it.

So as we read this book, let's step out of our "peanut butter and cracker" mentality and utilize our Christian resources—the riches of the Kingdom.

"Fear not, little flock, for it is your Father's good pleasure to give you the kingdom." (Luke 12:32, RSV)

1
WHO AM I?
The Need for Spiritual Identity

Who am I?

This is one of the questions most often asked by women today. The fast-changing world gives us so many identities that we often feel lost as to who we really are. Often, we have more facets to our lives than we can comfortably handle.

Who am I? Where do I belong? We all feel the need to belong, to be a part of a greater whole—a family, a tradition.

Today many of us are researching our family history to establish a sense of belonging. We travel back to family beginnings in the hope that it will help shore up today's shaky foundations—anything to give us more stability as the world reels in progress and technology about us.

And it is a good thing to trace one's family roots.

My friend June Gilmer spends hours digging in musty records of libraries for nuggets of information that will tell her something about her ancestors. She carries on volumes of correspondence with other researchers and travels to old cemeteries, courthouses, and family reunions all over the nation—all for bits and pieces of information that will help put together the jigsaw puzzle of people from her past.

June says she identifies with the stories of the struggles and triumphs of her early settler ancestors as she finds out who they were, where they came from, where they settled, and how they lived.

Of course it is important and comforting to know our physical heritage, but our spiritual identity and heritage are even more important. The frailties of physical things change or are lost, but our spiritual identity is ours forever. Understanding and affirming our identity as children of God give us an inner strength, a positive image, and a sense of belonging that can be found no other way.

The other day I got out a favorite faded tintype—a picture of my great-grandmother Anna Maria Lehr. It brought to mind her life—and her deep faith.

The picture shows her standing—a little stiffly in a long black skirt and white shirtwaist—in front of a little sod house on the flat prairie. This was the house that Anna Maria and her husband, William, built when they homesteaded on the part of the western prairie that was then called Indian Territory. (Today the family still owns the original homestead, which is now in the panhandle of Oklahoma.)

As I look at the picture, I think of the hardships that Anna Maria and her family endured and the sacrifices they made.

The family came to that part of the Great Plains and settled on wild and unknown land miles from any settlement. It was a dry land, hot and dusty in the summer, with a scarcity of drinking water. In the cold windy winter the sod house never got warm and food became scarce and dangerous illnesses often occurred. Then there was always the possibility of Indian raids.

Anna Maria, like the women who came before and after her, held many titles. She was wife and mother, homemaker, cook and nurse. She was weaver and seamstress, dairymaid and candlemaker. She was teacher to her children, not only of reading and writing but of the Bible, music, and manners. When her husband was away and she was left alone with her children, she became protector and huntress.

Anna Maria was also gardener and canner and preserver of food. Her family's life depended in part on her garden. She broke the sod, planted the garden in the blistering sun, and kept the plants alive with buckets of water she carried from the creek a half mile away.

Then she also worked beside her husband in the fields, settling the bundled-up children at the end of the rows where she could keep an eye on them.

When the rare travelers came by in their covered wagon, Anna Maria was the gracious hostess. She covered the rough boards of the table with her precious linen tablecloth and got out her fine china (which she had carried in the covered wagon wrapped in patchwork quilts). She set a table worthy of Mrs. Vanderbilt, serving with flair the venison stew and black bread.

Often William would be gone a week or more on hunting trips for food, and she and the children were left alone. One time a band of drunken renegades tried to break in and this not-quite-five-feet-in-height pioneer woman ran them off by shooting a rifle that was nearly as tall as she was.

There was no doubt about it, Anna Maria was a woman of great courage—and faith. With all her jobs and titles, I found that her spiritual identity, as a child of God, was the glue that held everything together.

For Anna Maria's well-used and marked-up Bible tells the story of her faith. On one of the front pages I read:

I, Anna Maria Lehr, hold steadfast to the following:
1. *I am a child of God and he loves me without measure.*
2. *God speaks comfort and help to me. I am never alone.*
3. *I have the right of spiritual inheritance.*

In these three statements, I found the secret to Anna Maria's life. Although she had many cares and responsibilities and as a woman lived under the most miserable and dangerous circumstances, Anna Maria knew who she really was.

She had no problem with her spiritual identity, for she "held steadfast." She knew she was a child of God and affirmed it, and that kept everything in her life in proper place and order.

Anna Maria held firmly to these precepts all her life. She lived to be ninety-five and never wavered. As a youngster I remember sitting beside her as she read her Bible while she slipped me pink peppermints. She had retained perfect eyesight at the age of eighty-nine and enjoyed reading a psalm without her glasses to anyone who came by.

Let's explore Anna Maria's three affirmations one by one.

1. *I am a child of God and he loves me without measure.*
As we establish our spiritual identity nothing gives us a firmer

foundation in every area of our life than recognizing that we are children of God. We are his beloved.

The psalmist tells us: "What is man, that thou art mindful of him? . . . For thou hast made him a little lower than the angels, and hast crowned him with glory and honor" (Ps. 8:4–5).

The Bible tells us about our spiritual nature when it says we are made in the likeness and image of God (Gen. 1:26). Then it explains that God is a Spirit and we must worship him in Spirit and in truth (John 4:24). What a beautiful way to show that our eternal self is linked to God!

One of the great missions of Jesus was to explain how the spiritual Kingdom of God is with us. He shows us how this is our link to the Infinite that enables us to transcend the purely physical.

Too often it is difficult for us, as adults, to accept our position as a child of God. It means shedding our facades, sophistication, cynicisms, and masks and coming as a child with open faith and trust. For we know that children do not have any problem accepting love; they eagerly reach out and embrace.

That is why Jesus put such a great emphasis on "child" and "children." He said the citizens of the Kingdom of God were those who "became as little children." So when we are called children of God, it is a special title of the Kingdom. And as children of God, we are loved by him without measure.

Knowing and accepting God's love are two different things. Often we must study and meditate on this great truth until we can completely believe and assimilate it within us. And when we come to the point of true acceptance of God's love for us, we are strengthened and our faith is built up for any challenge that lies ahead.

I have a friend Janice, who has just gone through the despair of divorce, losing her home and her family, sharing the custody of the children. Her life has been turned upside down and she says she feels as if she is in the center of a dark, angry storm.

And like many of us when we are in the midst of trouble and chaos, Janice cried out, "I thought God loved me!"

Of course God never stopped loving Janice. And he loves you and me, too—regardless of the circumstances.

But deep troubles and trials have a tendency to sever us from God. We get so caught up in the problem that we often forget our

Source. Or we become angry and bitter—and confused. That breaks the connection and this makes the situation even more difficult, for it takes away our lifeline.

It isn't until we realize that our salvation lies in reconnecting to our Source that we awake and realize what has happened. We have allowed an enemy to come in and steal our resources.

As Janice took her walk in one of the deep valleys of life, she found she needed much study and prayer time before she could reestablish her identity and reopen the line to her Source. Then God's love and comfort could come through to her in the midst of upheavals and grief.

Then my friend Janice, like believers before her, found that God's love flooded her soul with strength and comfort. For God is the angel in the lions' den (Dan. 6:22), the fourth man in the furnace (Dan. 3:25). In fact, that is where most of us meet him—at the point of our greatest need.

A statement that my great-grandmother wrote on another page of her Bible means much to me. After a long winter of severe suffering and sorrow she could still say:

> Circumstances of life might have tried to crush me, but never for one moment have they removed one jot of God's love from me.

2. *God speaks comfort and help to me. I am never alone.*

Anna Maria's second statement says that when we truly surround ourselves with the comfort of God's presence we are never alone.

I remember a time in my life when everything seemed to go wrong. Everything I attempted had gone sour and I felt as if my life were bouncing off a brick wall of frustration and delay. Then financial difficulties had piled up so high they seemed to strangle me, and physical problems were so severe I was ordered to bed.

What was I to do? I was at a point of desperation. Most of us have been to this place sometime in our life, where it seems everything humanly possible has been done and there is no place to turn.

Except to God.

For suddenly I realized that I was trying to do everything myself. Where was my faith? Circumstances had blinded me.

What about the Scriptures I had been repeating? Were they just words or did I really believe them and what they stood for? Could I feel calm and poised, believing that God was here, in my situation, even when all about me it seemed dark—and even hopeless? So again I said:

"The LORD is my shepherd; I shall not want." (Ps. 23:1)

"I will say of the LORD, He is my refuge and my fortress: my God; in him will I trust." (Ps. 91:2)

How many times I had said these words, because these Scriptures were old favorites and some of the first Scriptures a Christian learns.

But this time as I said them I held on, grasped them to my heart, and meditated on the principles involved. The Lord was my shepherd, my leader; he cared for me and I should want for nothing. I would be given what I needed—if I could only trust and see through the circumstances of the moment. And God was my refuge, my fortress, the castle built on the rock that couldn't be moved. I would trust in him—completely.

So did I believe or didn't I? Yes, I did—even though I didn't know what the next moment would bring. But wasn't that what trust was all about? Trusting that the next moment, hour, day, year was in God's hands?

As I prayed and meditated, I released the problems and allowed the words to become lifelines leading directly into my innermost being, beyond my subconscious. I felt as if I had a direct link to another dimension. I put God in charge—and I meant it.

As I was lying there, a warm feeling came over me. I felt as if I were covered with a warm blanket of liquid love. An inner knowing accompanied my feeling, assuring me that all was well. God was in his heaven and all was right with the world. It was such a strong feeling that no one could have convinced me differently.

I turned over in bed with this feeling of comfort flooding my spirit and dropped off into a comfortable and healing sleep.

The next morning I awoke refreshed, and the feeling of pure love was still with me. There was no anxiety, worry, or even concern. I felt as if I had been given a gift—a gift of faith and grace. And I had.

Later, when I read these words by the eighteenth-century

Swiss theologian Johann Kaspar Lavater, I knew he had had the same type of experience:

> I have enjoyed many of the comforts of life, none of which I wish to esteem lightly: yet I confess I know not any joy that is so dear to me, that so fully satisfies the inmost desires of my mind, that so enlivens, refines, and elevates my whole nature, as that which I derive from religion—from my faith in God. May this God be thy God, thy refuge, thy comfort, as he has been mine.

And my problems? Did they disappear by a miracle? Well, yes and no. When I look back I find they sort of dissolved—as the mist does when the sun comes out.

First they disappeared from my mind. Now they were still there in the outer world, but I had no anxiety about them. They were just impersonal challenges that I *knew* would be solved.

My problems did disappear as the weeks went by, mostly through ideas given to me when I demonstrated a willingness to listen to the voice within me, recognize the opportunities when they came, and do the work involved.

So through the worst of times I found that God had comforted me, spoken to me, and helped me.

I was never alone. He was there all the time.

3. *I have the right of spiritual inheritance.*

"We are children of God, and if children, then heirs, heirs of God and fellow heirs with Christ." (Rom. 8:16–17, RSV)

Anna Maria's third statement shows she knew she was an heir, for her spiritual identity made her a child of God with the riches of inheritance.

We are always a first-generation inheritor—a daughter of God, for God has no grandchildren. Each one of us must come to the position of inheritance by our own free will.

Very few people of Jesus' day understood him or the teaching that he brought to the world. The people were looking for a king who would assert himself physically—rally the troops, wage war and crush and conquer the enemy.

Instead, they found a king who preached love and talked about a kingdom that was not of this world (John 18:36). The inheritors of this Kingdom were those who sought the Kingdom first—and then everything else would be added (Luke 12:31).

Throughout this book I will explore the many ways Christian resources can help us in our lives and the spiritual inheritance that is ours. As we learn about our inheritance we will find that a deeper awareness of God always restores, renews, enriches, and sustains us. For following Christ's teachings and ways of love brings a well-balanced relationship into our life, not only with God but also with our fellow human beings.

The late Dr. Walter C. Alvarez, who was one of my favorite people, called Christianity a "healthy religion." Dr. Alvarez was an able physician who was given a special insight and understanding of human nature. He wrote many books, both for medical students and laypeople, and also wrote a newspaper column for many years in which he dispersed his special brand of medical common sense and wisdom.

Dr. Alvarez was a compassionate man who had a special understanding of the overworked wife and mother. He wrote about her often and described her as having several young children, too little sleep, and so many demands that she was strained beyond her physical capacity.

Dr. Alvarez was famous for writing a "special prescription" for this wife and mother. He would hand it to her husband and say that if the prescription was followed, it would save the family thousands of dollars in hospital bills later on.

The prescription read:

> Rx: Spend mornings resting in bed for the next six weeks.

When Dr. Alvarez was near the end of his career, having spent over fifty years medically treating and observing human beings, he was asked for a "recipe" for a good life. This is what he gave:

> A feeling of self-worth, a satisfying job, peaceful sleep, love, laughter, good music, and a healthy religion.

A healthy religion? What was a healthy religion? When Dr. Alvarez was asked, he said it was the religion that Christ brought—pure and simple, without man-made coverings. In his autobiography he later said, "When we get back to the simple religion of Christ—then we have something that we can accept and live by."

Dr. Alvarez was so right. The teachings of Christ are healthy and are never a crutch but an enhancer—a way to build human potential to its highest level.

When we affirm our spiritual identity, we negate the separation from God that began in the garden with Adam and Eve, for we move into union with God through an act of faith.

For we are then reconnected to our Source. We are no longer what D. Elton Trueblood called the "cut-flower civilization"— one that has been severed from its roots.

For we have come home.

Augustine expressed it this way many years ago when he said, "Thou hast made us for Thyself, O God, and our hearts are restless until they rest in Thee."

And the psalmist sang: "For he satisfieth the longing soul, and filleth the hungry soul with goodness" (Ps. 107:9).

RESOURCES

You can use the following resources as a basis for meditation and prayer to affirm your Christian identity and inheritance. Work not only with the words but with the deep principles underlying the words.

TO BEGIN WITH, WE KNOW
 We are children of God, and if children, then heirs, heirs of God and fellow heirs with Christ. (Rom. 8:16–17, RSV)
AND
 We are all the children of God by faith . . . and heirs according to the promise. (Gal. 3:26, 29)
THEN WE ARE TOLD OF OUR INHERITANCE
 Fear not, little flock, for it is your Father's good pleasure to give you the kingdom. (Luke 12:32, RSV)
AND
 They that seek the LORD shall not want any good thing. (Ps. 34:9)
FOR
 God will meet all our needs according to his glorious riches in Christ Jesus. (Phil. 4:19, NIV)

SO THEN WE CAN SAY WITH OUR WHOLE HEART

The LORD is my shepherd; I shall not want. (Ps. 23:1)

NEXT WE FIND STRENGTH

In all these things we are more than conquerors through him who loved us. (Rom. 8:37, RSV)

AND WE CAN SAY

I can do all things through Christ which strengtheneth me. (Phil. 4:13)

And I will say of the LORD, he is my refuge and my fortress: my God; in him will I trust. (Ps. 91:2)

FINALLY WE ARE TOLD

Be ye therefore followers of God, as dear children; and walk in love. (Eph. 5:1–2)

AND HOLDING HIS PROMISES WITHIN US, WE CAN SAY

In the multitude of my thoughts within me thy comforts delight my soul. (Ps. 94:19)

AND WE ALWAYS KNOW

The LORD will not cast off his people, neither will he forsake his inheritance. (Ps. 94:14)

FOR

He satisfieth the longing soul, and filleth the hungry soul with goodness. (Ps. 107:9)

AND

Goodness and mercy shall follow me all the days of my life: and I will dwell in the house of the LORD for ever. (Ps. 23:6)

WHILE WE HOLD TO THIS GREAT PROMISE

Lo, I am with you alway. (Matt. 28:20)

2
WHO IS MY SOURCE?
The Need to Understand God's Majesty

God's Front Yard

When the children were small, we loved to lounge in the backyard hammock and watch the first stars of the evening appear.

As dusk crept over the land, stars by the hundreds, then thousands, began to twinkle. They hung in the dark-blue Texas sky like sparkling diamonds, so vivid that we felt we could reach up and pluck them.

In fact, that was what three-year-old Renée would attempt to do as she ran about the yard carrying an imaginary basket. She filled it with "twinkles" and presented it to her daddy when he came out to join us. She explained that she had "picked the twinkles in God's front yard."

Thirteen-year-old Dwight, already the serious scientist, would give us some facts about the vastness of God's universe as we all watched the night sky together.

Dwight told us that the distances in the sky were so far apart that astronomers measured distances by light-years—the distance that light travels in one year at 186,000 miles per second. This makes one light-year approximately six trillion miles.

He also told us that even the nearest star outside our solar system, Alpha Centauri, is 4.3 light-years away. It would take a spacecraft faster than any we have today over 850,000 years to reach this star.

Dwight explained that our solar system—the relatively small

star called the sun and its nine planets—is part of a galaxy called the Milky Way. The Milky Way contains 300 million to 400 million stars and is 100,000 light-years across.

And that's not all. Astronomers say there are at least 100 billion galaxies like ours. And the average distance between galaxies is about 3 million light-years.

The figures of the vastness of God's universe can boggle the mind. In fact, these are distances the human mind has difficulty comprehending.

When my family and I were in the backyard studying the night sky, we were doing what people have done since the beginning of time—looking up at the heavens to get some sense of the awesomeness of God's creation and the majesty of God.

The psalmist understood this when he said, "The heavens declare the glory of God; and the firmament showeth his handiwork" (Ps. 19:1).

Compared to what is out there, we know so little about the universe. We have walked on the moon, but the distance we have gone when compared to traveling to Alpha Centauri is like comparing a little over a second to 4.3 years.

Just as it is difficult to comprehend the vastness of space, so is it difficult for our finite minds to comprehend the Infinite—God, our Creator. The psalmist expressed it this way: "Such knowledge is too wonderful for me; it is high, I cannot attain unto it" (Ps. 139:6).

The Old Testament uses beautiful imagery to attempt to explain God. He travels on the rays of the morning, through the roar of the thunder, and in flashes of lightning. He flies about on wings of the cherub and sometimes rides on the wind. His voice is like the roaring of many waters and he lives in the canopy of the heavens where he has named each star.

And we are told his laws are immutable and his goodness and mercy are forever.

The Qualities of God

In order to understand more clearly our resources, we Christian women must reexamine what we believe about our Source.

Our belief in God cannot be weak and wavering, nor even halfhearted. It must be strong and firm and definite.

24

Reviewing the three qualities of God will help us put the majesty of God in proper perspective and strengthen our belief and faith.

1. *God is omnipotent*—he is all-powerful. There is nothing God cannot do. He has unlimited authority and influence.

All power belongs unto God. (Ps. 62:11)

"Great is our Lord, and of great power: his understanding is infinite." (Ps. 147:5)

"The voice of the LORD is powerful; the voice of the LORD is full of majesty." (Ps. 29:4)

"He ruleth by his power for ever." (Ps. 66:7)

2. *God is omniscient*—he knows all. There is nothing God does not know. He possesses unlimited understanding, awareness, and insight.

"O LORD, thou hast searched me, and known me. Thou knowest my downsitting and mine uprising; Thou understandest my thought afar off." (Ps. 139:1–2)

"His understanding is infinite." (Ps. 147:5)

"I know the things that come into your mind, every one of them." (Ezek. 11:5)

3. *God is omnipresent*—he is present and existent everywhere.

"Whither shall I go from thy Spirit? Or whither shall I flee from thy presence? If I ascend up into heaven, thou art there: If I make my bed in hell, behold, thou art there. If I take the wings of the morning, and dwell in the uttermost parts of the sea; even there shall thy hand lead me, and thy right hand shall hold me." (Ps. 139:7–10)

As we study the three qualities of God, it helps us understand his greatness and majesty. For then our God is not too small. When we begin limiting God, we limit ourselves and our resources. Therefore we must keep our mind on the expansive, everlasting, and all-encompassing qualities of God.

As we learn about God and his power, we head toward great discoveries. There is no journey in the world as exciting as the journey inside us as we learn and grow.

For our Source is limitless.

Who Did God Say He Was?

When God spoke to Moses from the burning bush, Moses asked God who he was and what his name was. If Moses was going to lead the Hebrew people out of bondage as God had asked him to, Moses wanted to be able to tell them who had sent him.

So God told Moses: "I AM THAT I AM. Tell them I AM sent you."

God's description of himself could also be translated: I WILL BE WHAT I WILL BE, for God was describing himself as "That which is continual being."

Another way we could define this is to say that God was telling us that *he was all that ever was, is, and will be.*

That is just about as good a description of God as our human minds can understand.

How Jesus Defined God

Jesus, the Son, defined God, his Father, in a revolutionary but perfect way—the way of love.

He said the love of God, the Father, for his children was so great that words could not express it. He said if a human father wants the best for his children, just think how much more love the heavenly Father has for his children. (Matt. 7:11.)

When Jesus was asked what was the greatest commandment, he said there were two:

1. "Thou shalt love the Lord thy God with all thy heart, and with all thy soul, and with all thy mind, and with all thy strength."

2. "Thou shalt love thy neighbor as thyself." (Mark 12:30–31)

The love of God as expressed by Jesus is so vast and wondrous, how can we explain it? If we took all the love of every tender, caring mother that ever lived and multiplied it by millions and millions, we would have only a small portion of God's love.

The words of Jesus constantly remind us: "This is my commandment, That ye love one another, as I have loved you" (John 15:12).

26

The Secret Place Where We Go and Meet God

Be still, and know that I am God. (Ps. 46:10)

I once visited the home of a very wealthy woman. Lydia's home was a showplace of fine furniture, antiques, rich and colorful Oriental rugs, heavy crystal chandeliers, and expensive and rare collections of art.

Lydia was involved in many charities and was in demand as a speaker all over the world. She was on the board of several major companies and had investments throughout the country.

I was awed by the color and richness of her home. In every corner there were treasures she had collected from her travels— ivory, jade, Fabergé eggs, etc.

We were talking about how she found time for all her activities. "Come," she said. "I will show you my favorite room."

Her favorite room. What could top the opulence I had already seen?

When Lydia opened the door I was surprised to find a small, plainly furnished room with bare floors. There was a desk, several chairs, and a plain Shaker rocker. Two small bookcases were on the far wall.

"Here is where I come to read my Bible and to study and pray," Lydia explained. "This is the place I can meditate in calm and quiet. This is where the world is shut out and I can touch my Source and refresh myself. Then my spirit is renewed and I am ready to face the fast-paced world again."

We all have a secret place inside us where we can go and meet God, a place where we can leave the world behind and become reenergized, refreshed, and renewed—where God can speak to us and we can hear him.

There is a great truth in our relationship with God in the words, "Be still, and know that I am God." "Be still" comes from a root word meaning "quit striving," "give up," and "let go."

It is only when we stop and become calm, relaxed, and peaceful that the Inner Voice can speak to us.

Then we can be with him in the secret place of the Most High.

The psalmist understood this when he said, "He who dwells in the secret place of the Most High shall remain stable and fixed under the shadow of the Almighty [whose power no foe can withstand]" (Ps. 91:1, AMP).

The Wise Woman

THE WISE WOMAN
She who knows not
and knows not she knows not—
She is a fool—shun her.

She who knows not
and knows she knows not—
She is simple—teach her.

She who knows
and knows not that she knows,
She is asleep—awake her.

BUT
She who knows God
and knows that she knows—
She is wise—Follow her!

Abigail was a successful businesswoman who seemed to have it all. She was vice-president of one of the largest banks in the South, and had money, prestige, and honor. She wore designer clothes, lived in a smart townhouse, and drove a customized Porsche.

Who needed God? Not Abigail. She delighted in calling herself an atheist and prided herself in getting this far all by herself. She needed no one. Hadn't she proved it?

Suddenly life soured. Abigail lost control of one area of her life. The evening drinks she had taken to "calm her" had ensnared her. She found herself an alcoholic.

When her alcoholism became so severe that it affected her work, Abigail set about in her efficient way to find help. She tried biofeedback, hypnosis, aversion therapy, and other methods of behavior modification, but nothing worked.

Finally a doctor told her that the only avenue he knew left was Alcoholics Anonymous.

"Isn't that where you have to believe in God?" she asked.

"Well, perhaps," the doctor answered. "At least you have to believe in a Higher Power—God as you know him."

"Well, I don't know him and I don't intend to," Abigail replied.

The more she researched about AA, the more she found out they got results. And since she was the practical businesswoman and she needed something that worked, she decided to attend a meeting.

"And I don't intend to believe in God," she told the members.

"That's all right," they answered. "You can believe in the group. Just put your faith in AA. The organization. Many do that until they begin to believe and grow."

Believe? Grow? Abigail had news for them. No one was going to make her believe anything she didn't want to.

Months went by and even though she attended some AA meetings, and called on the people for help continually, she took one step forward and three back. Why wasn't it working for her?

Again they gently told her she had to believe in something higher than herself. She had to reach out beyond herself. Her spirit had to stand on tiptoe and reach up while she admitted she was powerless to do anything about her problem.

Since Abigail was now in a desperate condition she agreed—but only if she could use AA, the organization, as her Higher Power. After all, the people were kind and it seemed harmless. Besides, nothing else had worked.

So when Abigail reached out to Something Higher than herself, the situation changed. The impossible was being done. Little by little she began to take more steps forward than backward.

As time went on, she was so grateful for her progress that when someone in AA gave her a little booklet that contained the love chapter from the Bible—the thirteenth chapter of I Corinthians—she agreed to read it.

As Abigail read the verses, she was surprised to learn that the words reminded her of the loving friends at AA who had helped her.

She read how you could be the greatest and wisest and know all mysteries, but if you didn't have love, you were nothing but a loud noise.

She read that love was patient, kind, and long-suffering. Love is never envious or boastful. It is never haughty but always helpful. Love does not act unbecomingly. It is not touchy or

fretful or resentful. It bears up under anything and always believes the best of every person.

Love never fails. It is always there to hold you up.

As Abigail read, she remembered the times she had stumbled
and fallen in drunkenness and called out for help. The group
never complained or condemned no matter how many times she
had reverted to being a sloppy drunk. They just sat beside her
until she sobered up. Someone was always there to hold her
hand, even to hold her head as she vomited. They wiped her
brow and saw her through the agony of the trembling and the
shakes. And when it was all over, they spoonfed her broth to give
her strength.

There was never a word of reproach. They never criticized.
They were always willing to give her another chance. Kind,
patient—and loving.

Suddenly a light turned on inside Abigail.

Was that what God was all about? *Was love God's other name?*
The more she thought about it, the more she realized it was so.
Now she knew who God was.

> He was all the friends at AA who loved and helped her—
> and more.
> He was all those who never condemned her—and more.
> He was all those who never gave up on her—and more.
> He was all those who rejoiced in her new beginnings—
> and more.

Abigail felt something in her spirit take off and soar. She knew
she had touched God and would never again be the same.

"The fool hath said in his heart, There is no God." (Ps. 14:1)

But the wise say: "I will praise thee, O LORD, with my whole
heart." (Ps. 9:1)

RESOURCES

When you use the following resources in meditation and prayer,
they will open your mind to the majesty, love, and holiness of
God. The more you can envision the greatness and goodness of
God, the more your life will be touched by his Presence.

These resources can also be used when you are faced with challenges and situations that seemingly have no solution. They put your mind on the greatness of your answer rather than in the mire of the problem. This allows God's grace to come into your life and do its perfect work.

AS WE MEDITATE ON THE MAJESTY AND GOODNESS OF GOD WE KNOW

In the beginning God created the heaven and the earth. (Gen. 1:1)

SO WE

Stop and consider the wondrous works of God. (Job 37:14, RSV)

FOR

Yours, O LORD, is the greatness and the power,
and the glory and the majesty and the splendor,
for everything in heaven and earth is yours.
Yours, O LORD, is the kingdom;
you are exalted as head over all. (I Chron. 29:11, NIV)

Your throne was established long ago;
you are from all eternity. (Ps. 93:2, NIV)

AND

The law of the LORD is perfect. (Ps. 19:7)

You are my rock and my fortress. (Ps. 31:3, NIV)

FOR WE KNOW

God is light, and in him is no darkness at all. (I John 1:5)

SO

You, O LORD, keep my lamp burning;
My God turns my darkness into light. (Ps. 18:28, NIV)

AND SINCE

We know that in all things God works for the good of those who love him. (Rom. 8:28, NIV)

WE CAN SAY

If God is for us, who can be against us? (Rom. 8:31, NIV)

FOR GOD TELLS US

I am the LORD, the God of all mankind. Is anything too hard for me? (Jer. 32:27, NIV)

AND HE PROMISES US

I will instruct you and teach you in the way you should go;
I will counsel you and watch over you. (Ps. 32:8, NIV)

AND AS JESUS, THE SON OF GOD, HAS PROMISED
> I am come that you might have life, and that you might have it more abundantly. (John 10:10)

AND JESUS FURTHER REMINDS US
> Love one another, as I have loved you. (John 15:12)

FOR
> He that loveth not knoweth not God; for God is love. (I John 4:8)

AND
> By grace are ye saved through faith; and that not of yourselves: it is the gift of God. (Eph. 2:8)

SO WE KNOW
> If the Son shall make us free, we shall be free indeed. (John 8:36)

THEN
> Say among the nations, "The LORD reigns!" (Ps. 96:10, RSV)

3
THE WILL TO BELIEVE
The Need for Belief and Faith

Choices of Faith

As Christian women, we know that the happy, productive, and fulfilling Christian life is rooted in our belief and faith. The more we study and learn, the more we find that our victories are based on our faith, but more than that, they are based *on the depth of our faith.*

> Skimming the surface won't do it.
> Being lukewarm or fence straddlers won't do it.
> A passion for a deep belief and trusting faith is needed.
> We must set our will to believe, regardless of circumstances.

I remember the first time I paid close attention to the words: *"Without faith it is impossible to please God."* (Heb. 11:6, NIV)

My, I thought. That's not mincing words. It puts faith right out there as the deciding factor. It is the requisite in our relationship with God.

The rest of the verse explained why:

"Because anyone who comes to him must believe that he exists and that he rewards those who earnestly seek him." (Heb. 11:6, NIV)

Now, that makes sense. How can I believe in God before I believe he exists? So, in the spiritual realm belief and faith bring God into my life.

The more I studied, the more I realized there were steps of the will we must take before we can begin to have deep faith. We have to learn how to make continual conscious choices—correctly.

In our daily physical world, we often take faith for granted. Before I sit down I don't agonize over whether the chair is going to hold me. Unless I see something that alarms me, I just sit. I cross the street knowing the motorist's red light will hold the traffic until I reach the other side. I drive over bridges, fly in planes, take elevators, turn on the water faucets—all on automatic faith.

But it isn't like that in the spiritual realm.

Oh, yes, we made a strong commitment of faith in the beginning, but that is just the beginning. In the spiritual realm our mind is structured in such a way and the duality of conditions confronts us in such a way that we must stay alert and reaffirm our faith many times a day by making a choice.

Joshua, when he was talking to his people, said:

"Choose you this day whom ye will serve." (Josh. 24:15)

Then he added:

"But as for me and my house, we will serve the LORD." (Josh. 24:15)

If we could make this choice once and for all or even practice it until it becomes as automatic as brushing our teeth or driving a car, it would be easy. But it doesn't work that way in the spiritual realm.

We are put in myriad situations daily where we are confronted with a choice. Will we choose:

> Faith or worry?
> Trust or terror?
> Belief in ourselves or belief in inadequacy?
> Love or dislike—even hate?
> Understanding or intolerance?
> Joy or unhappiness?

Sometimes we find that not making a choice is a choice. We allow ourselves to drift into the negative kingdom without really making a conscious choice. It is as if we were on a boat that we stopped steering and allowed the current to carry into the wrong fork of the river. Then our resources are stolen from us before we realize it, and we have to fight our way back out of a negative cycle.

We always have a choice. We can set our will toward belief. It is up to us. We *can* keep from goofing up our garden.

When a Christian woman with a deep and knowing faith believes, the glass is never half empty, for with God the glass is full to the brim and running over.

And therein lies the difference.

What Is Faith?

Often we have difficulty understanding what faith really is. Faith is being certain of something that we do not see. It is the intangible that brings the tangible into being.

My favorite definition of faith is found in the Amplified Bible:

> "Now faith is the assurance
> (the confirmation, the title-deed)
> of the things [we] hope for,
> being the proof of things [we] *do not see*
> AND THE CONVICTION OF THEIR REALITY—
> faith perceiving as real fact
> what is not revealed to the senses."
> (Heb. 11:1, AMP; emphasis added)

Faith is reliance and trust in a loving Father. When we rely on the Presence of God, we become calm and positive no matter what the situation. We can be secure in the realization that there is nothing—no situation—that is beyond his power.

We all are given a measure of faith (Rom. 12:3) and we can increase our faith by hearing the Word of God (Rom. 10:17). As we stand fast in faith, we feel strength and courage within us and we become assured of God's power and love. We stand firm and know that all is well.

1. Faith is the belief in the greatness and majesty of a loving God, who cares for his children.

2. Faith is the belief that God means what he says in his word.

3. Faith is the belief that God wants to answer our prayers more than we want to ask them.

4. Faith is the belief in the wisdom of God, who will answer

our requests in the best interests of everyone concerned.

And how much faith do we need? Jesus said only as much as a tiny mustard seed.

Jesus used the mustard seed as a symbol of increase because the seed begins no bigger than a speck. When the mustard seed is planted and nurtured by the soil and the sun and the rain it grows into a huge plant the size of a small tree.

In the same way, what we plant in our consciousness with a small amount of faith, if nurtured, will flourish and grow to maturity.

Activating Our Faith

Be ye doers of the word, and not hearers only. (James 1:22)

We often get caught in the subtle difference between belief and faith. Just because we believe doesn't necessarily mean we have faith. The difference is sometimes hidden, but it is there.

A traveler was once lost in the desert and was dying of thirst. He finally crawled up to an oasis with a real sparkling pool of water.

This water could save his life. He believed this with all his heart.

Slowly he crawled to the edge of the pool and lay there, repeating over and over: "I believe this water will save my life."

He reached out his hand and dipped it into the water. Again he said: "I believe this water is my salvation. I believe this water is what I need to live."

Of course what he said is true. His belief was correct; the water could save his life.

But he never went beyond his belief; he never took a drink. And so he died.

When we act on our belief, speak words of faith and trust, and bring our faith into active energy, blessings happen. Sometimes it means "holding our faith" in a strong and decisive way, other times it could mean physical action.

God's universe is rich with potential and possibility. One door closes and another opens. There are always resources at hand to fill every need.

A House Undivided

All things are possible to him who believes. (Mark 9:23, RSV)

When we have faith our actions, words, and thought should conform to that belief.

One time I was attempting to activate my faith. An unhappy situation had arisen among family members and I was praying for peace, order, and tranquillity.

My young daughter asked: "Mom, are you sure you are believing? Your shoulders are sure slumped."

With true faith, everything we do—even the position of our body—should be in conformity with our faith. Everything we say, think, do, and live. A house divided is not true faith.

When we pray believing, it should be an affirmation of life—a positive and strong expression of our belief that God hears and answers prayer. God is in the midst of the situation and knows what is best for all.

How to Stand Fast in Faith

Watch ye, stand fast in the faith . . . be strong. (I Cor. 16:13)

Stand fast therefore in the liberty wherewith Christ hath made us free, and be not entangled again with the yoke of bondage. (Gal. 5:1)

What does standing fast in the faith really mean? How does standing fast release us from the yoke of bondage? Why is "standing fast in the faith" one of the secrets of the overcoming Christian life?

To stand fast is to know with a deep inner conviction that regardless of circumstances there is an immeasurable power for good at work. It means to have more faith in God and his goodness than in what we see in the circumstances. It is knowing that God, All Good, is working behind the scenes.

Unless we stand firm, our faith can be continually buffeted about by the world—people, conditions, news we hear—any circumstances.

When our faith becomes eroded and weak, we can lose the

battle. Then we are like Peter walking on the water, becoming afraid and looking down. He sees the high waves and the angry water, and losing faith, he begins to sink. But Jesus caught him, just like the Christ within us can lift us up.

I used to read the story about Noah and the ark and wonder why God instructed Noah to build the ark with a window way up near the roof that was only eighteen inches high. The more I thought about it the more I realized that way Noah could see only the sky.

He could only look up. He could not see the raging waters and the high waves that threatened to sink the ark.

And that is what we must do. We must continually look up. We must have faith in God's power, which is greater than any appearance of evil. With God all things are possible. He has the divine ability to restore and adjust all conditions. The power of God works through us and through every circumstance to bless.

The "Dig Deeper" Times

This is the victory that overcomes the world, our faith. (I John 5:4, RSV)

Yes, you say, that is all well and good. But you don't know *my* situation. It is impossible.

We all have times in our lives when we must dig deeper, when we need all the faith we can muster. Sometimes it is not so much that we need to stretch more faith muscles as that we need to know how to use what we have.

If we dwell on our inadequacies, we become "locked in." If we attempt to force faith with our will, that is wrong, too. Faith is setting the will toward God and then relaxing in the knowledge that God is at work. If we don't set our will toward faith in a strong, firm way, we can easily drown in the bits and pieces of pity, doubt, fear, and confusion. Often it takes much faith and patience to hold on.

I remember one time in my life when things were exceptionally challenging—and that's putting it mildly. What was worse, I believed how bad things were and went along with the negative tide. The more I believed my circumstances were the final word, the more I lost my resources. So things worsened.

For now I had added depression, fear, and doubt to my list of challenges.

And unforgiveness.

For what happened tested all my spiritual strength.

I had just spent three years regaining my health through medical help and prayer, and through a series of senseless mishaps all my progress had been wiped out. Seemingly, I was in a worse condition than before.

I was what the doctors call a "clinical ecology" or environmental patient.

The doctors said that years before I must have been exposed to industrial chemicals, insecticides, or weed poisons that seemed to have wiped out the ability of my body to cleanse itself of conditions in the environment that most of us take for granted. For instance, exposure to car and truck exhausts, paint fumes, tobacco smoke, or perfumes was like poison to my body and could send me to the hospital in serious condition.

Thanks to much prayer and fine medical help, after several years I had reached the place where I could function nearly normally in the environment.

But my progress was all wiped out when workmen, in the process of installing an electrical heating unit in our home, created several fires, smoke-damaged our home, and exposed me to gas and chemicals. I was sent to the hospital in worse condition than before.

After I was released from the hospital I spent seven months on oxygen in an "environmentally pure" room and it would take several more years before I could see progress.

During this time I was looking so strongly at circumstances that my mind had difficulty believing that the situation could right itself.

For, as I have mentioned, the prognosis was not in my favor. Humanly. It was so bad that a friend told me (yes, like Job I had those friends) that Jimmy the Greek wouldn't even give me odds.

So when I turned to God I had to work at my faith daily, hourly, even minute by minute, until everything inside of me believed that God was with me and there was an answer.

As I went along month after month, I found I had to do a lot of forgiving, cleaning my spiritual house to unclog my Lifeline.

Then I had to use my resources with repetition, insistence, command, until I felt a response in my heart.

However, the adversary continually tried to steal my joy. Most of the time I could not go on my feelings but had to hold on to my resources. And when things were especially rough, I found that if I went back to basics, using my resources as shown in Chapters 1 and 2 of this book—affirming my identity and the majesty of God—I routed the enemy more easily. For I was shoring up my foundations and building on solid rock.

Finally the situation changed. The victory was won. And the victory was sweet. And I give thanks for it.

I felt like singing with the psalmist: "Truly my soul waiteth upon God: from him cometh my salvation" (Ps. 62:1).

Overcoming a Faith Robber

We are assured and know that [God being a partner in their labor], all things work together and are [fitting into a plan] for good to those who love God and are called according to [His] design and purpose. (Rom. 8:28, AMP)

In talking to Christian women, I find that one faith robber is common. Often we allow an imperfection or mistake in our life to weaken our faith. Perhaps we have stumbled—"missed the mark" and didn't live up to our best expectations for ourselves.

Then we get into a syndrome—even after we have asked for forgiveness—where we feel God is far, far away. He doesn't hear us. He is no longer close.

God has forgiven us, but we haven't forgiven ourselves. And that, of course, separates us from our Source.

The sad part is that we are in the syndrome because we have made our loving and forgiving God too small.

I remember hearing Corrie ten Boom speak several years ago and she told a story that always stayed with me.

Corrie, as you remember, was the Dutch Christian woman who survived the German concentration camps to become a world traveler, writer, and speaker.

It seems that Corrie was visiting a Swiss school for weavers. Everyone was busy, bent over their looms, moving the shuttles back and forth in just the right way to weave the beautiful cloth.

"What happens if you make a mistake?" Corrie asked one of the apprentices. "Is the material ruined? Do you have to throw it away?"

"Oh, no," said the pupil. "We tell the teacher. He is a great artist and he shows us how to work our mistakes into the pattern so it has even greater beauty than before."

And why shouldn't this also be so in our lives? Aren't we told that God makes all things work together for good? Even our mistakes can be woven into the tapestry of life to make a beautiful pattern.

But God Meant It for Good

Another faith robber is when we find ourselves in a situation that was brought about by the evil actions of another—the havoc caused by drunken drivers, muggers, robbers, etc.—any situation where one person is put in a position to hurt another. Such a situation is so senseless we reel at the horror of it.

This makes our life take a sudden twist, turn, or change that seemingly takes us into impossible territory. Often we feel it has put us into the desert more than forty years. We find ourselves thinking, How could any good come from this?

If we hold fast in faith and put God consciously in charge of the situation, we can find that good can come from our journey.

One of my favorite verses in the Bible comes from the story of Joseph. You remember how the brothers of Joseph, because of jealousy, sold him into slavery and he was taken into Egypt.

As the years went by, Joseph rose in favor and was finally made governor of Egypt. Through God's guidance he had been informed of a drought that was coming, so he had the people store up the grain for the lean years.

When the famine became intolerable in the land of Joseph's brothers, they came to Egypt to buy grain. Joseph not only sold them grain but revealed who he was and invited them and his father and the rest of the family to Egypt to live in plenty.

When Joseph's brothers fell on their faces before him and begged his forgiveness for what they had done, Joseph said: "You intended to harm me, but God intended it for good." (Gen. 50:20, NIV)

God can take any situation that was meant for evil and turn it into a triumph for good.

Mustard Seeds and Mountains

For if you had faith even as small as a tiny mustard seed you could say to this mountain, "Move!" and it would go far away. (Matt. 17:20, TLB)

How often have we read Jesus' words that faith can move mountains? Do we really believe it? A mountain?

Pastor Ray Crawford and his church proved that faith and prayer can really move mountains.

It seems that Pastor Crawford's church had just built a new sanctuary on eight acres of property which was one-half mountain and woods. They had dug out the front part for the church. Now the church backed up to a "mountain" over forty feet high.

Then the church found out the city wouldn't issue them a parking permit unless they had more ground for parking, which meant shaving down that forty feet of mountain and moving it away.

That seemed impossible. Even if it could be done, the church didn't have the money to pay to bulldoze that mountain and haul it away. They were barely surviving the way it was.

But wait! Wasn't there something in the Bible about Jesus saying you could pray with faith and tell the mountain to move?

So the next Sunday morning Pastor Crawford reminded his congregation of this promise of Jesus. You could say, "Hey, mountain! Move!" and it would be so. Did they believe or didn't they?

Pastor Crawford was very logical about the situation. "The Word of God says if we have faith we can move a mountain. It talks specifically about *a* mountain. We have *a* mountain. It needs to move."

Then the pastor said: "Anyone who really believes this promise, be here Wednesday night. We will have a special mountain-moving prayer service."

Then he warned: "If you don't believe—even a little doubt—don't come. Please examine yourself and if you have any problem

42

believing this promise, stay home. We want only true mountain-moving believers!"

As you can imagine, the Wednesday night congregation was sparse. And even some of the believers voiced that they could not visualize how God was going to move that mountain.

The pastor reminded them that moving that mountain was God's part—all they had to do was to have faith that it would be done. Meanwhile they could show their faith by gathering prices and estimates for turning the land under the mountain into a parking lot. When the Lord moved the mountain they would be ready.

A few days later the pastor received a call from the telephone company. They were in the process of erecting a new building in a swampy area on the other side of town and they found they needed much fill dirt. Could they please have the mountain in back of the church?

So during the next few months the telephone company hauled away over forty thousand square yards of fill dirt, for which they insisted on paying. Not only that, when the mountain was moved, they leveled the ground and prepared it for paving.

When the church paid for the paving, they found they had money left over. Not only was the mountain moved, the parking lot paved, but there was money left over to put into the church coffers.

No matter what our mountain—the greatest of challenges—it can be moved with faith.

RESOURCES

Faith resources are doubly important in the Christian life because faith and the study of the Scriptures is the foundational key to the Kingdom. As we affirm and reaffirm our resources, we find that our faith will grow.

NOW

Faith is being sure of what we hope for and certain of what we do not see. (Heb. 11:1, NIV)

FOR

Without faith it is impossible to please God, because anyone who comes to him must believe that he exists and that he rewards those who earnestly seek him. (Heb. 11:6, NIV)

AND WE ARE TOLD

God hath dealt to every man the measure of faith. (Rom. 12:3)

WHILE WE CAN INCREASE OUR FAITH, FOR

Faith cometh by hearing, and hearing by the word of God. (Rom. 10:17)

AND WE REALLY NEED VERY LITTLE FAITH, FOR WE ARE TOLD

If you have faith as small as a mustard seed, you can say to this mountain, "Move from here to there" and it will move. Nothing will be impossible for you. (Matt. 17:20, NIV)

AND WE ARE ALSO PROMISED

Whatever you ask for in prayer, believe that you will receive it, and it will be yours. (Mark 11:24, NIV)

WE FIND THAT FAITH AND FEAR ARE INCOMPATIBLE

Jesus saith, Why are ye fearful, O ye of little faith?

Then he arose, and rebuked the winds and the sea; and there was a great calm. (Matt. 8:26)

AND EVEN WHEN OUR FAITH FALTERS, GOD IS STILL FAITHFUL

If we are faithless, he will remain faithful,

for he cannot disown himself. (II Tim. 2:13, NIV)

BUT WHEN OUR FAITH IS DEEP, WE ARE TOLD

You may ask me for anything in my name, and I will do it. (John 14:14, NIV)

AND

Fight the good fight of the faith. (I Tim. 6:12, NIV)

THEN WE ARE TOLD

Arise, go thy way: thy faith hath made thee whole. (Luke 17:19)

AND WE ARE GIVEN THIS GREAT PROMISE

I tell you the truth, anyone who has faith in me will do what I have been doing. He will do even greater things than these, because I am going to the Father. (John 14:12, NIV)

AND WHEN WE STAND FIRM IN FAITH, WE CAN SAY

I have fought a good fight,

I have finished my course,

I have kept the faith. (II Tim. 4:7)

4
GOD'S BOOK OF RESOURCES
The Need to Be Nourished by God's Word

The Bible—Our Sourcebook

For ever, O LORD, thy word is settled in heaven. (Ps. 119:89)

Once I was packing for a trip to Europe and since my luggage poundage was limited, I was attempting to fit everything into one bag.

My daughter, Renée, brought me my "book bag," a suitcase filled with favorite books that I usually carry on trips.

"I won't be able to take my book bag this time, Renée," I said. "All the space I have is this little corner of my suitcase." I pushed some clothes aside.

"But," I added, "nevertheless I am going to take a volume of poetry, history, biography, geography, songs, prayers, a guidebook—"

"But, Mother," Renée interrupted, laughing, "you won't have room for all of them."

"Oh, yes, I will," I said as I slipped in my Bible.

The Bible is all that and more. And the Bible is the Christian woman's Sourcebook for help, strength, wisdom, and power.

As we are buffeted on every side by the busyness of the world, with challenges presented to us that are continually stretching our faith and wisdom, we need the nourishment and guidance of God's word—daily.

The "God-breathed" wisdom of the ages that is in the Bible is awesome—a spiritual vortex and a reservoir of promises for better living in every way.

As we learned in the last chapter, the power, promises, and help in the Bible will work in our lives "according to our belief." It is up to us. The help is there if we wish to use it.

Understanding What the Bible Is

The Lord gave the word: great was the company of those that published it. (Ps. 68:11)

For years I only read parts of the Bible. I would stay with the familiar verses, because the moment I would stray to parts of the Old Testament where people killed each other, put out their neighbor's eyes, and stoned one another I was embarrassed.

How could a book that tells us to love one another, to love God and our neighbor, have such unsavory stories in it?

Then one day I realized that the theme of the Bible is the story of humankind's journey back to God from the separation in the garden. It shows the journey from very primitive beginnings where it seemed the primary goal of human beings was to extend their territory and kill their neighbor. The Bible doesn't mince words, cover up evil, or soften any steps of the record along the way. It tells it just like it is.

Fortunately there were always a few people along the way who heard the voice of God on their level of understanding. Noah, Abraham, Moses were some who tried to lift humankind higher.

Then I realized that the Bible is a collection of over ten thousand events—both good and evil—that record the activities and the actions of people who responded to a living faith when they found God revealing himself to them on the level of their comprehension.

I found that the Bible gives us direct, clear, and precise teachings about our search for God—and God's answers. There are essays, stories, and sermons on the nature of human beings, the nature of God and God's plan for humankind, and the meaning of life. Through historical narrative, geographical studies, prayers, praise, poetry, parables, and raw drama the Bible teaches, expounds, and directs.

The Bible contains the greatest prayers ever written, the greatest pleas to God—and the greatest answers.

The Bible shows humankind's deliverance from bondage in

thousands of ways, on every level of understanding and for every type of person.

Finally, the Bible comes to the ultimate: Jesus' revolutionary revelation of love—for God, for yourself, and for your neighbor.

It is important to remember that the Old Testament shows humankind's release from *outward bondage;* the New Testament shows humankind's release from *inward bondage*—showing the overcoming by Jesus Christ to set us free.

That is the wonderful good news of the gospel.

Coming to the Bible with a Need

Heaven and earth shall pass away, but my words shall not pass away. (Matt. 24:35)

Learning about the Bible is a lifetime study, for the material is so rich and varied. You will find that the Bible is a "principle" book. And these principles are not just true because they are in the Bible. *But they are in the Bible because they are true.* In other words, the truths you find in the Bible are God's wisdom of the ages—tested by time.

You don't have to be a scholar to read the Bible. All you have to do is come with an open mind and a willing heart, willing to be led by the Holy Spirit.

How often I have come to the Bible with a need, and I will find a verse or a group of verses that literally jump out at me. I have just opened my Bible, am thumbing through and—look! the message is for me and the situation of my life at the time. It gives guidance, comfort—sometimes admonition—whatever is necessary. I am always amazed at the power and wonder of the deep message the words contain.

Then several days later I look at the same words and they are just Bible verses. And I think, Did I get all that help from those words? And I look back with awe at what had happened to me.

Other times I can pluck Scriptures out of my memory for a certain need and they will act the same way—special. They are also the right words highlighted for my needs at the time.

And other times the word is like a seed, as Jesus showed us in the parable of the sower (Matt. 13:18–23). When the word falls on fertile ground and is planted deeply in the heart, it grows and

47

increases and comes to maturity producing a harvest of results. We must remember that the word we read and hold in our heart will produce according to how we receive it, believe it, and stand firm on it.

How to Study the Bible

Open thou mine eyes, that I may behold
wondrous things out of thy law. (Ps. 119:18)

There are many ways to study the Bible. We can study a verse, a chapter, a book, a theme or a subject—to name just a few. But no matter how you approach the Bible and study, it is always profitable.

1. *Bible Study for Quiet Devotional Times*

I love to sit down quietly with a pen and a notebook and study the Bible during devotional times. I begin my study with prayer, repeating the above Scripture and asking for enlightenment.

Whether I am studying a book, a chapter, or even a verse I meditate on the following:

a. Who is speaking?

b. What is the main subject of what I am reading? Often I rewrite it in my language, making my own paraphrase.

c. What are the key verses? Often I copy verses to memorize.

d. What are the principles involved? What is the lesson or the purpose to be learned?

e. How can I apply this principle or lesson to my life today?

2. *Studying a Word, Subject, or Theme of the Bible*

"The word of the LORD is right; and all his works are done in truth." (Ps. 33:4)

Often I use a concordance and a Bible dictionary if I want to look up a subject or theme and study all the words pertaining to it.

For instance, there are more than five hundred references to *love* in the King James Version of the Bible. So by the time you have studied them all you have the grand concept of love from every viewpoint and meaning.

Or perhaps you are interested in the theme of Bible covenants. You will find every covenant in a concordance from Noah's (Gen.

6:18) to Abraham's (Gen. 15:18) to Jesus', the mediator of the new covenant (Heb. 12:24).

3. *Studying Bible Names*

"Whatsoever ye shall ask the Father in my name, he will give it you." (John 16:23)

Studying the names and their meanings in the Bible will open up the Bible in a new way.

We find that a name in the Bible designates the nature of the thing. Naming a person, place, or thing was an act of power.

For instance, Jesus' name meant savior: "Thou shalt call his name JESUS: for he shall save his people from their sins" (Matt. 1:21).

Often in the Bible when a person reached a certain spiritual understanding of God, his name was changed. Abram (father of height) was changed to Abraham (father of multitudes). And when Jacob (supplanter) wrestled with the angel all night and was blessed, he had his name changed to Israel—prince of God.

Often names were given to prophesy that which was coming. For instance, the longest name in the Bible is a man's name, and was given to the son of Isaiah: Mahershalalhashbaz. This means "hasten the spoil, rush on the prey" and was given to show that the nation of Israel would be plundered by its enemies because of disobedience.

4. *Studying Numbers in the Bible*

Studying the numbers used in the Bible is another way to deepen understanding. For example, the number "forty" stands for a time of completion.

We find that Moses had three periods of forty years each in his life. The first forty years was spent in Egypt, the next forty years was spent "on the backside of the desert" preparing for his mission in life, and the last forty years was the mission: leading the children of Israel through the desert and receiving the laws of God.

Moses went up to the mountain and stayed forty days and forty nights. Jesus spent forty days and forty nights in the desert. It rained during the flood forty days and forty nights, etc.

To Study and Learn God's Word Is to Grow

For the Word that God speaks is alive and full of power—making it active, operative, energizing and effective; it is sharper than any two-edged sword, penetrating to the dividing line of the breath of life [soul] and [the immortal] spirit, and of joints and marrow [that is, of the deepest parts of our nature] exposing and sifting and analyzing and judging the very thoughts and purposes of the heart. (Heb. 4:12, AMP)

We find that as we come with an open and receptive mind and show a willingness to learn life becomes exciting. Not only that, we find that the more we stretch spiritual muscles, the more life becomes a glorious adventure.

> Think back to the place you were in understanding
> five years ago.
> Think of the place where you are right now.
> Project to where you will be in growth and love five
> years from now.

It can be awesome. For if we truly have increased in understanding, we will be able to see and feel a difference. Are we more loving? More tolerant? More forgiving? More poised in grace? Do we live from a center of calm and serenity?

When we look about us, we see the universe is geared to growth—to expansion. And on earth, have you ever watched the will to grow of a seed? It is planted and immediately energy begins to stir and it starts sprouting. Have you ever thought of all the power a seed needs to poke through the soil?

I remember one time we planted zinnia seeds, which are light and look like little pieces of straw. They germinate quickly and want to get about the business of growing.

However, we hadn't raked our soil properly and huge clods of dirt were lying about. But that didn't bother the little sprouts. We watched with amazement as they pushed the huge clods of dirt aside, clods that weighed thousands of times what the little sprouts weighed.

The energy behind the thrust to grow was greater than the obstacle.

That is our natural state. To grow and glow and learn more and more. And the beautiful thing is that we can never study and learn more about God without growing in understanding and love.

All the promises in the Bible were given to us to use and to help us grow, but we must remember to stand on the promises in faith.

Someone once said the promises were like the Emancipation Proclamation—it was there, even as a law on the books, but it wasn't until a hundred years later that the people who had been freed really claimed the promise and made it work.

Personal Scriptures of Faith

Thy word have I hid in mine heart. (Ps. 119:11)

The following are a few examples of combining favorite Scriptures of faith to make them personal to you.

The Lord is my shepherd, I shall not want and he has given his angels charge over me and I will dwell in safety. (Ps. 23:1; Matt. 4:6; Prov. 21:31)

I know the word of the Lord endureth for ever and heaven and earth shall pass away, but his words shall not pass away. (I Peter 1:25; Matt. 5:18)

The Lord is with me and will deliver me and shall guide me, for he has heard my prayers and will answer them. (Jer. 1:8; Isa. 58:11; Ps. 6:9)

I can do all things through Christ who strengthens me and he goes before me and makes the crooked places straight, for with God all things are possible. (Phil. 4:13; Isa. 45:2; Mark 10:27)

God knows what I need and when I put my trust in him, I shall be safe. (Matt. 6:32; Prov. 29:25)

"Never Again's"

I found that when I use "never again's"—throwing out what I don't want in my life and then affirming the positive Scripture—they reached the depth of my consciousness more easily.

The following are self-image enhancers:

1. NEVER AGAIN will I agree to spiritual bondage, for I am free

because "where the Spirit of the Lord is, there is liberty." (II Cor. 3:17)

2. NEVER AGAIN will I submit to feelings of unworthiness, for I am "created in Christ Jesus unto good works." (Eph. 2:10)

3. NEVER AGAIN will I express self-condemnation, for there is "no condemnation to them which are in Christ Jesus." (Rom. 8:1)

4. NEVER AGAIN will I say I am a failure, for "I can do all things through Christ which strengtheneth me." (Phil. 4:13)

5. NEVER AGAIN will I show frustration, confusion, anxiety, or apprehensiveness, for I have within me "the peace of God, which passeth all understanding." (Phil. 4:7)

6. NEVER AGAIN will I give in to the challenges of life, for "greater is he that is in me than he that is in the world." (I John 4:4)

7. NEVER AGAIN will I allow opposition to intimidate me, for "if God be for me, who can be against me?" (Rom. 8:31)

8. NEVER AGAIN will I feel insecure but I will believe in myself, for "the LORD shall be my confidence." (Prov. 3:26)

9. NEVER AGAIN will I express a lack in any area of my life for "God shall supply all my need according to his riches in glory by Christ Jesus." (Phil. 4:19)

10. NEVER AGAIN will I admit to disbelief or doubt, for "all things are possible to me that believeth." (Mark 9:23)

RESOURCES

The following resources are to affirm and establish more firmly the infused power and strength of the Word of God in your life.

I have found that this set of resources is also excellent to encourage and confirm inner strength before prayer.

IN THE BEGINNING WE KNOW

By the word of the LORD were the heavens made; and all the host of them by the breath of his mouth. (Ps. 33:6)

AND ALSO

In the beginning was the Word, and the Word was with God, and the Word was God. (John 1:1)

AND WE KNOW

The word of the LORD is right; and all his works are done in truth. (Ps. 33:4)

For whatever God says to us is full of living power: it is sharper than the sharpest dagger, cutting swift and deep into our innermost thoughts and desires with all their parts, exposing us for what we really are. (Heb. 4:12, TLB)

ALSO

It is written, Man shall not live by bread alone, but by every word that proceedeth out of the mouth of God. (Matt. 4:4)

AND HE TELLS US

If ye abide in me, and my words abide in you, ye shall ask what ye will, and it shall be done unto you. (John 15:7)

AND WE REPLY

Lord, . . . thou hast the words of eternal life. (John 6:68)

Quicken me, O LORD, according unto thy word. (Ps. 119:107)

Thy word is very pure; therefore thy servant loveth it. (Ps. 119:140)

I rejoice at thy word, as one that findeth great spoil. (Ps. 119:162)

Thy word is a lamp unto my feet, and a light unto my path. (Ps. 119:105)

For ever, O LORD, thy word is settled in heaven. (Ps. 119:89)

AND GOD SAID TO US

Let your heart hold fast my words; keep my commandments, and live. (Prov. 4:4, RSV)

Attend to my words; incline thine ear unto my sayings. Let them not depart from thine eyes; keep them in the midst of thine heart.

For they are life unto those that find them, and health to all their flesh. (Prov. 4:20–22)

AND WE REPLY

I will bow down toward your holy temple
and will praise your name
for your love and your faithfulness,
for you have exalted above all things
your name and your word. (Ps. 138:2, NIV)

5
PRAYER REFRESHMENT
The Need for Communication of the Spirit

Prayer

Pray without ceasing (I Thess. 5:17)

Things happen when Christian women pray, for they know that prayer is the most powerful force for good on earth.

Prayer changes situations and people.
Prayer changes unhappy wasted lives to fulfilled productive people.
Prayer changes sickness to health.
Prayer changes poverty to abundance.
Prayer changes loneliness to love.
Prayer changes emptiness to joy.
There is nothing, absolutely nothing, that prayer cannot do.

In the earlier chapters we have discussed four foundational Christian needs:

1. Recognizing and affirming our spiritual identity
2. Understanding God's goodness and majesty
3. Faith and belief
4. God's Sourcebook, the Bible

Now we are going to focus on prayer, which puts it all together and projects into our outer world.

For in the Christian woman's life, prayer is where the action is. Prayer makes things happen. Through our prayers God moves on earth and gets things accomplished.

God wants to answer our prayers, for he is always ready to express himself.

Prayer is·one of the few things in the world for which there is no substitute. Prayer is unique and nothing can take its place.

We know prayer is communication with God. It is the touching of our spirit with God's Spirit, but, more important, prayer is our alignment with God and his goodness.

Prayer always changes things. Not one word can be uttered in prayer without changing the one who prayed, if only in a minute way.

So not one word spoken in prayer is ever wasted.

Prayer Is Refreshment of the Spirit

No matter what type of prayer we pray, prayer is always refreshment for our spirit. It revitalizes, renews, and rebuilds.

For when we pray, we touch the Source of our inspiration as well as the Source of our good.

In this chapter I will be focusing on "asking" prayers, prayers that answer needs in our lives. For God communicates with us at the point of our need—in our arena of life—where we live. And prayer is the key to the abundance of the Kingdom.

Why shouldn't prayer lead us to God's bountiful blessings? Aren't we told, "Ask, and ye shall receive" (John 16:24) and "in him we live, and move, and have our being" (Acts 17:28)?

As we turn to God in prayer, and feel his presence, we realize with absolute certainty that he is with us, guiding us and reassuring us and moving through us as he uplifts us and brings answers.

We Are Commanded to Pray

My prayer life used to be sparse, even though I was a committed believer, because I thought God didn't want to be bothered with my problems. Who was I to ask for help and for answers to my needs?

Or at the time I did pray, if I didn't get immediate results, I gave up. Since I was praying with a question mark, and really didn't expect to get results, that is exactly what I got.

So I reserved my prayer time for rare and formal occasions.

But as I deepened my study, I found it shouldn't be like that. For as Christians, *we are commanded to pray. And receive.*

For we are told:

"Pray without ceasing." (I Thess. 5:17)

"Men ought always to pray, and not to faint." (Luke 18:1)

"Watch and pray." (Matt. 26:41)

"Ask, and ye shall receive, that your joy may be full." (John 16:24)

Could any directives be plainer?

And every name and attribute of God implies that he hears and answers prayer: a living God—all-knowing, all-hearing, all-loving; Infinite Wisdom; Limitless Power; a loving Father, Helper, Comforter.

God is continually urging us to receive from his abundance, his stockhouse of blessings in order to fulfill his purpose to his creation.

Aren't we told he is a "rewarder of them that diligently seek him" (Heb. 11:6)?

And the psalmist called him, "O thou that hearest prayer" (Ps. 65:2).

We Are Commanded to Ask

Then I found that not only are we commanded to pray but we are commanded to ask for what we need. For we are to eliminate any fears that we might have that we are presumptuous.

Nothing could be plainer than the following Scriptures:

"Ask, and ye shall receive." (John 16:24)

"Ye have not, because ye ask not." (James 4:2)

"For every one that asketh receiveth." (Matt. 7:8)

"Ask, and it shall be given you." (Matt. 7:7)

"If ye shall ask any thing in my name, I will do it." (John 14:14)

"And all things, whatsoever ye shall ask in prayer, believing, ye shall receive." (Matt. 21:22)

Certainly this shows that we are to ask. We are to reach out in prayer for our needs.

The word for *ask* used in these Scriptures is not the word used to mean "inquire" *(eperotao)*. It is the word *aiteo*, which means to ask for, to desire, to call for—always in the sense of asking for something.

These promises of asking and receiving have no limits put on them. We are to ask for what we need: peace, health, money, understanding, wisdom, companionship, etc.—no matter how trivial or how awesome.

There is no limit in time. These promises are based on eternal and unchanging principles, as valid today as when they were written.

So that means there is no situation too hopeless, no challenge too great for a Christian. The answer awaits us. As we ask and pray we are led from the darkness of despair to the light of God's grace.

My friend Ruth wasn't afraid to ask God for her needs. She would tell me she received as great a joy out of praying and asking as she did when she received answers. For when she asked, the moment she prayed, she knew, in her spirit, that the answer had already come.

Ruth was a youthful seventy plus and some of her prayers—for her grandchildren and great-grandchildren—were for years ahead.

"I might not be here when all the answers to my prayers come true," she explained, "but I can rejoice now because it is an accomplished fact."

It is an accomplished fact. Thank you, Father. With those words Ruth ended every prayer. In her spirit she had already established it so by prayer.

I remember one time I told Ruth about a particularly difficult challenge in my life. We wanted to send our son to college, but our finances seemed hopelessly inadequate.

Ruth clapped her hands in delight. "Oh, good! Here is another opportunity for God to reveal his greatness. He is always seeking to pour more of himself through us. Since the challenge is great— what a wonderful answer you will receive!"

And that's the way it worked out. Step-by-step, semester-by-semester, the need was always met. Mostly at the last minute. In fact, we didn't have eleventh-hour miracles. We had "11 hours, 59 minutes, and 59 seconds" miracles. We marveled.

I remember Dwight saying, "Mom, our prayers are always answered, but it is a little nerve-wracking. I wish God wouldn't deadline it so!"

But the answer always came. It was an accomplished fact. Ruth's favorite verse:

> "Fear not, little flock;
> for it is your Father's good pleasure
> to give you the Kingdom."
>
> (Luke 12:32)

Seeking Answers through Prayer

When we ask and seek and receive answers through prayer, God doesn't answer haphazardly. For his laws are immutable and just and he is always ready to answer if we align ourselves properly. The greater our understanding, the more our prayers bear fruit.

The rest of this chapter will cover areas of "asking" prayer— the steps we take as we actively seek answers through prayer. (The added dimension of the prayer of praise and thanksgiving will be discussed in the following chapter.)

Establish Your Desire

> *Delight yourself in the LORD*
> *and he will give you the desires*
> *of your heart.*
>
> (Ps. 37:4, NIV)

Our desires are valid and healthy and can even be called "nudges from God." If a desire doesn't run counter to Biblical principles, to the law, or hurt another, it is a holy desire.

When we pray, our desire should be clear and precise in our mind. We should never feel vague or confused about our desire. If we do, we should pray a "clarifying and guidance" prayer. Then we work with our desire until it is sharp and definite in our mind. And I find that as I clarify desires, I learn much about my desire—and myself. Often my desire changes, goes in another direction—or I find it wasn't a valid desire at all!

Let me tell you about a woman with a strong desire and just as strong a faith in God—two qualities that make for success.

Mary Kay Ash is the founder and chief officer of the multimillion dollar corporation that bears her name. She has over 200,000 women who are company representatives of the Mary Kay line of cosmetics.

Years ago, Mary Kay founded the company with a deep, heartfelt desire, but she didn't know she had the desire until she began writing about it.

It happened this way. Mary Kay had worked for another direct selling corporation, had been successful and had learned the principles of selling. Now she wanted to write a book that told other women how to sell, even how to begin their own company.

The more Mary Kay researched and wrote, the more she found she was outlining goals and expressing desires of her own heart. Why not begin her own company?

The more Mary Kay wrote, the stronger her desires became and the clearer her goals were. The desire became so strong she could feel it, taste it—it permeated her very being. Now all she needed to do was activate her faith and begin.

So Mary Kay established her company with much prayer and faith in God. And from the very beginning she taught every employee how to be enthusiastic, work hard, and have faith in God.

Mary Kay found that faith in God was so important that she has her employees establish their priorities God first, family second, and company third. For Mary Kay has never forgotten who her Source is. We shall discuss more about Mary Kay and her unique company in Chapter 11, "Work, Goals, and Dreams."

How strong should our desire be?

Do you remember going swimming on a hot summer day and everyone was splashing water on each other and teasing about? Suddenly the play got a little rough and someone pulled you under or held your head under water in fun.

How badly did you want air?

That's how strong our desire should be.

Total Belief

As thou hast believed, so be it done unto thee. (Matt. 8:13)

For as he thinketh in his heart, so is he. (Prov. 23:7)

Believing is so important in "asking" prayer that it must be stressed again and again.

One way to strengthen belief is to make sure we have a desire that our mind will accept. I have noticed that when I have problems with believing, it pays to go back and clarify my desire.

Then I realize that I am working with a desire my mind won't believe. So I pray in vain. For instance, I can easily believe that I could find a job by next week, but it would be difficult for me to believe I would find a million dollars by next week.

One of the best ways to make belief stronger is to use the power of visualization. When I use the power of my imagination and bring the picture of my desire into focus, my belief is strengthened.

Our imagination is tricky. When it works against us, it can bring us much misery, as in worry or a continual pessimistic outlook. But when we capture our imagination and harness it and make it work for us, tremendous things happen.

One of the first times I used visualization in prayer was when my daughter was continually ill with inflamed ears. Neither doctors, nor medicine, nor prayers had seemed to help, and the condition was in danger of becoming chronic.

I also realized that because the condition had gone on so long, it was difficult for me to visualize her well.

One day was especially difficult. She had been in pain all day. That evening I was sitting by her bed where she was turning and tossing in her sleep. I was trying to pray, but I felt I was getting nowhere.

But like mothers everywhere, when they see a great need for a child they love, I decided to get serious in my prayer. For I felt something had to be done. That situation had gone on long enough. Somehow I had to break my belief in the illness and turn my belief to God—and health.

Several days earlier I had been reading about using the picturing power of the mind in prayer. So I began to visualize what I desired: pink and healthy ears, a clear eardrum, no fluid or infection problem. My daughter was completely whole. I saw her in my mind running toward me, smiling and saying: "Mom, my earache is gone! I am well!" I visualized the healing love and power of Jesus Christ surging through her healing her—NOW!

It took me several hours visualizing in this way over and over before I could say I really believed in my heart and could give thanks for the healing, knowing it was accomplished. And when I looked over at her, she was sleeping peacefully.

The next morning she had no problem, and by the week's end she was well.

When we visualize we are using the faculties of the mind to help us believe. So often I am asked, Isn't that what goal-oriented success books do? What is the difference using it in prayer?

There is much difference. One is using it without God and the other with God—in prayer. We can use the natural mechanics of the mind only. But when we use it in prayer, we are adding the spiritual dimension.

We know that programming the conscious and subconscious mind is a way to achieve. But with prayer, we are going one step farther. We are directing all the faculties of the mind toward the spiritual realm. We are turning to God where there are possibilities unlimited and prayer is answered in perfect order.

There is another interesting aspect of visualization. When you use this faculty of the mind in prayer, make sure your details are clear, in order, and definite—just as you wish the outcome to be. For as you think (visualize), so shall you receive.

We still chuckle about what happened to my friend Rachel when she used visualization in prayer.

Rachel and her husband, Bill, are graduates of Southern Methodist University. Their daughter, Laurie, was graduating from the same school. Laurie desired to attend Southern Methodist University Law School, but it was a year when there were overcrowded conditions and many students with excellent grades were being turned down.

Rachel did everything humanly possible to get Laurie enrolled, including adding the extra power of visualization to her prayers. As she prayed, she visualized Laurie graduating in cap and gown, standing beneath a sign that said "SMU." She did not use the words "Southern Methodist University"—just the letters SMU.

And that is exactly what happened. Laurie graduated from SMU, but this SMU stood for St. Mary's University!

Pray the Solution—Not the Problem

Unless we focus on what we want rather than on what we don't want, we can end up worse than before. For we are setting the problem in the cement of our belief.

When our mind is on the negative, zooming in on the trouble, emphasizing the dire situation, we never rise above the circumstances we are trying to overcome.

I learned this lesson many years ago from a dear Sunday school teacher, Mrs. Grayson, who had been in the hospital for some tests. She was teaching our class this particular Sunday, but was scheduled to go back into the hospital the next day.

Mrs. Grayson asked the class for prayer. We were all young and eager to help her, so we asked Darlene, who had a flowery command of language, to lead in prayer. For when Darlene prayed, molehills turned into mountains.

Darlene had carefully kept up with Mrs. Grayson's progress, so she knew all the details of the illness. Now she listed for the Lord all the aches, pains, symptoms in vivid medical terms, even including the doctor's dire prognosis.

"Stop!" Mrs. Grayson cried. She looked exhausted. "Darlene, I know you mean well, but if you continue praying and believing like that—I'll—I'll die!"

Then Mrs. Grayson gently explained that we were praying the problem rather than the solution. We were directing all our attention and the power of prayer to the illness rather than to healing and health.

Mrs. Grayson asked that we pray for her in this way:

> Visualize her whole and healed.
> See her well, laughing and happy.
> See the love and light of God flowing through her,
>   energizing her, revitalizing and healing.
> Surround her with the peace and harmony of health.
> Give thanks to God for her healing. See it done.

So all that next week we prayed for Mrs. Grayson in this manner. And despite the negative medical prognosis, Mrs. Grayson became well.

Even though Mrs. Grayson's healing was proof of the benefits "praying, believing, and seeing the solution" could bring, it was many years before I really took this concept seriously.

And practiced it.

It can't be stressed too often that we can know about all the bounty of the Kingdom, have all resources at our reach, yet, each one of us, personally, must put them into practice.

No one can do it for us.

Oh, we can have support in prayer and others can pray for us, but ultimately it is our free will that makes the choice.

Don't Dictate the Ways and Means of Prayer Answers

As for God, his way is perfect. (Ps. 18:30)

When we pray we should leave the means of the answer up to God.

We have found that if we get hung up in the concern and care of how the answer will come, we limit our prayer answers.

If you think your answer to prayer has to come from one person, one paycheck, or in a particular way, you are limiting your prayer by tunnel vision.

Often our mind can see only one way the answer could come when God has infinite possibilities. If we allow our finite mind to dictate ways and outcomes to the Infinite, we sabotage and short-circuit our prayer answers.

One of the most interesting answers to prayer is what happened to Rosemary, a young friend of mine.

Rosemary moved into an efficiency apartment that provided a stove and refrigerator but the only other furniture she had was a bed.

"I need a table and chairs," she said. "And I don't see how I can get it until my next raise in pay—about six months from now."

"Why don't you pray an 'asking' prayer?" I suggested.

"For a dinette table and chairs?"

"Why not? It's a valid need. And because you desire it so strongly, your answer will come quickly. If you believe."

Rosemary admitted that she had the need and a strong desire, but it was difficult for her to see how she could get the table and chairs before she had a raise in salary.

I explained how she was limiting herself because of her belief. The universe was full of tables and chairs and she should let God dictate the means of the answer.

Rosemary worked with this thought and finally said she could see how her table and chairs could come. "I'll probably get a chance to work overtime or a part-time job," she said.

I told her it was a good thing she was willing to work for the table and chairs, for that was one thing I felt was necessary in any prayer—the willingness to work if our answer came that way. But she was still limiting herself with her belief.

So she worked with her belief pattern some more and finally could see her answer coming from any direction. And then her prayer turned from one of "asking" to one of "giving thanks for the answer."

And Rosemary's table and chairs came in a delightful way.

A young couple, who had just bought a new home, was moving from the apartment complex in a rented truck. The truck broke down outside Rosemary's apartment. They asked to use her telephone to call the rental company to send out another truck.

It was a hot scorching day in July and Rosemary invited the couple in while they waited for the truck. She served them iced tea on the packing box she was using for a table.

When the truck arrived they found it was smaller than the one they originally had. So when the furniture was transferred from one truck to the other, they found that they didn't have room for some items.

Standing in the middle of the road was a pretty orange-and-tan dinette set.

Would Rosemary like to have it?

It seems that their new home had a built-in dinette booth and they were going to sell the table and chairs anyway. By the time they came back for it and put an ad in the paper and went through the bother of selling it, it wouldn't be worth doing. They noticed she didn't have a table and chairs, so would she like this set?

For free?

Be Willing to Work for What You Ask

Answers to prayers come in many sizes, forms, and shapes. Many times the answer comes in the form of an idea or an opportunity. Or a door opens in a new way.

Often these ideas and opportunities mean work and effort on our part. And we must be willing to do the work necessary.

Sometimes the answer to the prayer itself means taking on new responsibility. For instance, if you are praying for a new home, are you willing to assume the responsibility that home ownership means? Cleaning and taking care of a larger space. Keeping the yard in shape. Taking care of extra taxes, insurance, etc.

Unless we are willing to do what is necessary to bring about our prayer answer or assume the added responsibility, we pray in vain.

I know a woman who has been praying for years to publish a book, but she doesn't want to put in the long hours of hard work that is necessary to write one. She doesn't like the work involved in learning her craft: the loneliness, the discipline, the study that is necessary for a writer. She wants an "instant book" without having to do any work. So far this hasn't come about and her prayer goes unanswered.

Of course God can answer your prayer by bringing a free dinette set to your door as he did in Rosemary's case. He should never be limited. But if your answer comes in the form of an idea or an opportunity, you should be ready and willing to do your part.

So be alert.

Honor God with Your Request

If ye shall ask any thing [ANYTHING] in my name, I will do it.
(John 14:14)

How often we make our God too small. We don't have the courage to request what we really desire—or need. This happens especially if we desire something big, lavish, something that goes beyond what we have in our immediate world.

The story is told of a powerful king who was in a generous mood after a great victory. He told his subjects that they could come before him and ask anything they wished.

They all were so awed and afraid of the king that when they came before him, they asked for small favors: a sack of wheat, a bushel of potatoes, or a jar of honey.

All but one man. He said: "Sire, you are generous to give me the opportunity to ask anything—anything I want. So I ask for the forty-acre island of fertile land you have won that is just off the shore."

The room became completely still. All the servants and subjects held their breath. Surely this man would be killed for his audacity.

The king looked at the man for a long time. Now everyone knew for sure that this upstart would be beheaded.

But then the king broke into a big smile. He said: "At first I was shocked at the magnitude of your request. But then I realized that only a powerful ruler had it in his capacity and power to give someone an island. Your request is granted."

Honor God with your request—small, large—whatever you have faith for. The magnanimity of God exceeds anything our mind can grasp.

Don't Give Up

Ask, and it shall be given you;
Seek, and ye shall find;
Knock, and it shall be opened unto you.
(Luke 11:9)

Just before Jesus said these words, he was telling the story of a man who needed bread and came to a friend's house asking. The friend refused and it wasn't until the man continued knocking that the friend gave him what he wanted. Jesus said the man got his bread because of his persistence, not giving up.

When I think of persistence in prayer, I think of Brother Bev, his firm faith and his "hollow log" prayer time (G. C. Bevington, *Remarkable Miracles;* Logos International, 1973).

G. C. Bevington, or Brother Bev, was an itinerant preacher who walked about the countryside in southern Indiana and Kentucky about the turn of the century. He went wherever God led him, holding meetings in schools, in barns, or under a tree.

But Brother Bev would do as much practical help and work as he did preaching. He would often find God telling him to take over the household of a poor overworked farm woman with a passel of children. If she was sick, he would not only do her housework but would pray until she was well.

In those days a woman had her work and man had his, but Brother Bev didn't think it was degrading or demeaning to do housework. Therefore he often found himself cooking, baking, and cleaning house while taking care of all the children. He sang and prayed while he worked, and like Brother Lawrence of *Practicing the Presence* fame, he did everything for the glory of God, even washing dishes and diapers.

Brother Bev's life was full of answered prayer—and many miracles. His faith was simple and direct. When he saw a need, no matter what—food, sickness, shoes—he went directly to God.

And Brother Bev didn't fool around when he believed. He believed with his whole heart and soul and never gave up until the answer came.

Brother Bev had an unusual habit when he felt the desire to pray for someone, especially if the situation was very serious. He would go into the woods and find a hollow log and crawl in. There he would stay and pray until the answer came. He said sometimes it took him several days to "get his faith working" and "get himself out of the way."

But Brother Bev would hang on until he had the relief in his spirit that the prayer was answered. Often he would "see" the woman he was praying for get up out of her sickbed—well. Then he would relax and let go and crawl out of his log, knowing it was so.

We don't have a hollow log deep in the woods to crawl into to pray. Life is continually happening all about us. But we can build our ark, our strong pillar of faith and trust. And we can keep knocking until the answer comes.

Relax and Let God

There is a final step to "asking prayer" that is important.

There comes a time when we must relax, release our request to God and know that it is so.

It seems simple but it is often difficult because we want to keep on doing something, to work more, pray more, continue.

But there is a time to let go, to be still and know that God is working. For our answer can come in the quietness of being enveloped in a loving Presence that knows and fulfills our every need.

And this can also be the time for the prayer of praise and thanksgiving, which is what I will focus on next.

RESOURCES

The resources used in this chapter about prayer are some of the greatest and most powerful promises of the Bible.

These are not just words to a Christian woman, for these promises are given to us to use. And they will be activated in our life "according to our belief."

Reading them again and again will stimulate our belief and make our faith grow.

WE KNOW

LORD, thou hast heard the desire of the humble: thou wilt prepare their heart, thou wilt cause thine ear to hear. (Ps. 10:17)

For thou, Lord, art good, and ready to forgive; and plenteous in mercy unto all them that call upon thee.

Give ear, O LORD, unto my prayer; and attend to the voice of my supplications.

In the day of my trouble I will call upon thee:
for thou wilt answer me. (Ps. 86:5–7)

AND YOU TELL US

Call unto me, and I will answer thee,
and show thee great and mighty things,
which thou knowest not. (Jer. 33:3)

AND YOU ALSO SAY

Is any one of you in trouble? He should pray. (James 5:13, NIV)
Call upon me in the day of trouble: I will deliver thee. (Ps. 50:15)

FOR

The prayer of a righteous person is powerful and effective. (James 5:16, NIV)

SO WE ARE TOLD TO

Pray without ceasing. (I Thess. 5:17)

AND YOU FURTHER TELL US

Whatever you ask for in prayer, believe that you will receive it, and it will be yours. (Mark 11:24, NIV)

AND

Delight yourself in the LORD
and he will give you the desires of your heart. (Ps. 37:4, NIV)
SO
We ought always to pray, and not to faint. (Luke 18:1)
AND YOU PROMISE US DIRECTLY AND FIRMLY
If you believe, you will receive whatever you ask for in prayer.
(Matt. 21:22, NIV)
AND WE BELIEVE THIS GREAT PROMISE YOU HAVE
GIVEN
Ask, and it shall be given you;
Seek, and ye shall find;
Knock, and it shall be opened unto you:
For every one that asketh receiveth;
And he that seeketh findeth;
And to him that knocketh it shall be opened. (Matt. 7:7)
ALSO YOU HAVE SAID
If ye shall ask any thing in my name, I will do it. (John 14:14)
AND YOU EVEN TELL US
It shall come to pass, that before they call, I will answer. (Isa.
65:24)
For your Father knoweth what things ye have need of, before
ye ask him. (Matt. 6:8)
FOR WE KNOW
The eyes of the Lord are over the righteous, and his ears are
open unto their prayers. (I Peter 3:12)
FOR
He is a rewarder of them that diligently seek him. (Heb. 11:6)
SO IN THANKFULNESS WE PRAY
Our Father which art in heaven,
Hallowed be thy name.
Thy kingdom come.
Thy will be done in earth,
as it is in heaven.
Give us this day our daily bread.
And forgive us our debts,
as we forgive our debtors.
And lead us not into temptation,
but deliver us from evil:
For thine is the kingdom, and the power,
And the glory, for ever. Amen. (Matt. 6:9–13)

6
THE UNIVERSAL ANTIDOTE
The Need for Praise and Thanksgiving

The Universal Antidote

When a mother takes her baby to the pediatrician for a six-month or nine-month checkup, the nurse hands her a leaflet and tells her to read it carefully, because her baby's life could depend upon it.

The printed page gives warning and instructions about babies and poisons. It tells the parents to keep poisons away from the crawling, inquisitive baby. It explains that to a baby a poison could be anything from a dishwashing detergent to insecticides.

The leaflet further instructs how to call the poison control center and gives antidotes to various poisons. It tells the mother to go to the druggist and get a "universal antidote"—a mixture that counteracts and neutralizes many of the poisons that a child might ingest.

A universal antidote that counteracts and neutralizes.

We also have such a substance in the spiritual realm.

It is the prayer of praise and thanksgiving.

And it is the Christian's universal antidote that not only counteracts and neutralizes the ills of the world but also uplifts our spirits and has miracle ingredients built in.

Praise—A Sweet Fragrance

Praise and thanksgiving is the prayer that always carries a sweet fragrance, for praise and thanksgiving opens the windows of the heart and brings in the light and love of Christ. Praise builds an altar to God in our heart.

The principle of praise goes back as far as recorded history. We can imagine primitive man and woman standing and watching the sun rise on a beautiful world and silently giving thanks to Whatever Is Beyond.

Probably the most famous praise literature in the world is the Psalms of the Old Testament, for the Psalms are the devotional center of the Bible. They explore every facet of praise that arises from the human heart.

The Psalms say: "Let every thing that hath breath praise the LORD" (Ps. 150:6).

And in the psalms of King David, we find the honest and varied expressions of the human heart that lead up to praise. Sometimes we find the psalmist crying, sometimes he rails against heaven, sometimes he is depressed, but his emotions always lead to praising God—his Source of Being.

The psalmist says he will praise the Lord no matter what happens, for he knows that praise and thanksgiving keeps his soul pure, fresh, and holy as he goes about his daily living.

Even after great suffering and anguish, we hear the psalmist saying:

"I will sing to the Lord as long as I live. I will praise God to my last breath! May he be pleased by all these thoughts about him, for he is the source of all my joy" (Ps. 104:33–34, TLB).

Another time he says praise helped him realize:

"God's laws are perfect. They protect us, make us wise, and give us joy and light.
God's laws are pure, eternal, just.
They are more desirable than gold.
They are sweeter than honey dripping from a honeycomb.
For they warn us away from harm and give success to those who obey them." (Ps. 19:7–11, TLB)

In Everything Give Thanks

In every thing give thanks: for this is the will of God in Christ Jesus concerning you. (I Thess. 5:18)

When I first studied this Scripture and others similar that tell us to give thanks for everything, I thought: Everything, Lord?

So I did more studying and found that the prayers of praise and thanksgiving were foremost in the mind of religious thinkers. As I read their books and biographies and autobiographies, I found that praise was the spiritual fuel that kept them going.

Plutarch said, "The worship most acceptable to God comes from a thankful and cheerful heart."

Then the famous eighteenth-century English clergyman William Law said he found the surest way to happiness was to thank God for everything that happened. He said that by thanking God and praising him, we turn what happened into a blessing.

Charles Spurgeon said that there is a general end to our troubles when we see God's hand in every trial. And that pithy Quaker lady Hannah Whitall Smith said that praise turns trials into "chariots of triumph."

So, now as I studied I was beginning to get the message: The reason why we should thank God for everything.

For praise and thanksgiving turns a negative into a positive. It takes the situation away from the adversary, puts it under God's banner, and heads it for good. This went right along with one of my favorite verses: "You meant evil against me; but God meant it for good" (Gen. 50:20, RSV).

Why, I thought, if this really works, it can make a tremendous difference in my life. It can turn me from being a victim of what happens to me in life to a receiver of great potential. It can change a life full of troubles to one that is triumphant.

Then I realized that when we praise God for the situation "as is" we are trusting him to turn it around and head it in the right direction.

Then I found out another thing: praise is never in the past or in the future. It is IN THE NOW—THIS MOMENT. And we are lifted up. And God has the perfect solution.

But then I had another question: Why would God need our praise?

The more I thought about it, the more I realized that God doesn't need our praise. *But we need to praise.*

Our omnipotent, omnipresent, omniscient God of love has no ego to appease. He is unchangeable, immutable. But as we praise we establish our connection to him.

And so I came to the conclusion that praise and thanksgiving is the total and joyful acceptance of the present as part of God's loving and perfect will for us—when we put it under his banner. And which will work out for good.

Praising on a Hot Day in Texas

The first time I prayed the prayer of praise and thanksgiving was a day to remember.

It happened during the dog days of a hot Texas August. It can get so hot at that time of the year that not only can you fry an egg on the sidewalk, but old-timers say you can barbecue a whole brisket of beef.

It was 106 degrees that day. And both our hot-water heater and our air-conditioning unit had gone out, so I had two repairmen working in the heater closet, which was in the hall right off the master bedroom.

No one was in a good mood. We were hot and sweaty despite the iced tea and Coke I kept serving.

Throughout the day I was trying to pray a prayer of praise and thanksgiving, but I wasn't really getting anywhere.

It was late in the afternoon when the hot-water heater man came out and said the new gas water heater was installed and lighted and everything was O.K. Then he left.

I walked into the hot den and sat down in the maple rocker and began fanning myself with a newspaper. I was really trying to pray a prayer of thanksgiving, regardless of the circumstances, but it seemed I needed help.

So I opened my Bible flipping through The Psalms. I was aggravated at myself. If I couldn't praise and give thanks in a situation no more serious than what I was going through—just hot, uncomfortable, and inconvenienced—what would I do if a really serious situation arose?

So I garnered all my mind power and read the first verses I saw in the Psalms beginning with the word "praise":

"Praise ye the LORD. O give thanks unto the LORD; for he is good: for his mercy endureth for ever.

Who can utter the mighty acts of the LORD? Who can show forth all his praise?

Blessed are they that keep judgment, and he that doeth righteousness at all times." (Ps. 106:1–3)

73

Then I flipped a few pages further and read:

"Praise the LORD, all ye nations: praise him, all ye people.

For his merciful kindness is great toward us: and the truth of the LORD endureth for ever.

Praise ye the LORD." (Ps. 117:1–2)

Just then I heard an exclamation from Mr. Sawyer, the air-conditioning man. He came running into the den and fiddled with the thermostat.

"Mrs. Burroughs," he said. "I don't know what happened, but I just lost the wire in the wall that runs to this thermostat. I'll have to bring some special equipment tomorrow and fish for it."

He noticed my dismayed look.

"Oh, I can give you air-conditioning tonight," he said. "It's just that I'll have to put a temporary thermostat in the heater closet. Since your gas water heater is also in there, you'll have to leave the closet door open or it will get too hot and the thermostat won't work."

Mr. Sawyer went back to his work, shaking his head and mumbling: "I wonder what happened to that wire. That never happened to me before!"

Well, I thought, at least we will have air conditioning. But with that heater closet door open next to our bedroom, we would have to listen to fan motor and water heater noises all night long.

(You can tell by how I handled this situation that I had a long way to go to learn the principle of praise. And how desperately I needed it!)

In a short while Mr. Sawyer had the air conditioning hooked up and left, cautioning me to keep the heater closet door open.

When my husband came home about twenty minutes later, he smelled gas as he approached the heater closet. He immediately called the emergency department of the gas company who sent someone out within minutes.

The inspector found that the new water heater had a defect. A sealing ring had been left off, and gas was escaping at a fast rate.

He turned to me and said: "Lady, it's good that you had to have this closet door open so you could smell the gas. Otherwise, at the rate that gas was escaping, it could have pooled under the house and blown up the place!"

God Lives in Our Praises

We are told that God lives in the praises of his people (Ps. 22:3).

And wherever God resides, people and conditions right themselves.

When I really learned to add the prayer of praise and thanksgiving to my life, a spiritual door opened of such beauty, joy, and holiness that words cannot express it.

It must be experienced to be understood.

For in praising we do not run away from a situation or become Pollyannaish, but we acknowledge that God is our Creator and he is in charge. Then we are put in a condition of mind and will to hear, receive, and obey.

Henry Ward Beecher said that a thankful heart sweeps through the day like a magnet drawing blessings.

And that is true.

For the by-products of praise and thanksgiving are every good gift that comes down from above (James 1:17).

When we verbally use the praise principle, we are recognizing God's sovereignty in our lives and we affirm our willingness to put any situation in our life into his hands. Then blessings we receive come from our seeking first the kingdom and then all things are added (Matt. 6:33).

Praise Brings Light Into the Life

No darkness can lurk in the vessel filled with praise, thanksgiving, and gratitude. Any negative, whether doubt, anger, resentment, fear, envy, unforgiveness, cannot live in a person filled with the principles of praise.

Someone said that praise is an exterminator of devils. Praise keeps our mind on God and always brings peace into our life.

"Thou wilt keep him in perfect peace, whose mind is stayed on thee." (Isa. 26:3)

Praise brings the joy of willingness into our life. We know that God knows our need before we ask. And he also knows how we reached our present situation and what we need to do to change it.

Often in changing a situation there is a learning process ahead of us. When we praise we are putting ourselves into a receptive and willing state of mind so that God can work in our lives.

Then depression lifts, for in Isa. 61:3 we are told that we are given "the garment of praise for the spirit of heaviness."

Praise Breaks a Longtime Prayer Impasse

Do you have prayer areas in your life that you feel have been stalemated? Perhaps you have prayed for something or someone for a long time and nothing has happened.

Begin to release the problem with the prayer of praise. You will find a new release, a new joy, and a change in the situation. Many times I find that I either get an answer or have been praying in the wrong way or for the wrong thing.

The Praise Principle in Relationships

The following are some ways that the praise principle can help us in our relationships.

1. Are you locked in a will-to-will situation? If you pray a genuine prayer of praise, you will find that you stop manipulating and release and give God an opportunity. When we release we quit trying to make others fit into our ideas and molds. (This will be discussed in more detail in Chapter 9 on marriage.)

2. Are you faced with a challenge so huge that you are consumed with concern? Are you holding the person in fearful, anxiety-ridden prayers? Stop all "asking" prayers and release. Begin a prayer of praise and thanksgiving, knowing that the situation will work out in God's grace.

3. Do you really want to clean out hidden corners of your life? Begin praying the prayer of praise for an enemy. Is there someone you dislike, someone you have had problems with, or even someone who has hurt you deeply? Pray the prayer of praise to right the situation. You might have to approach this situation from several angles before you can truly pray. And until forgiveness comes. But just think of the exercise your ego is getting!

4. Are you living with some of the following phrases?

What could have been's
If only I'd's
Look what they did to me's

A praise phrase, such as used in the resource section at the end of this chapter, will make them scoot out of your life.

5. Are you meshed in fruitless activity, dead-end roads, and delaying tactics? I have found that the prayer of praise and thanksgiving can break us out of these negative and self-destructive cycles.

Praise God Just Because He Is God

To praise God just because he is God is the most wonderful prayer of all.

For we give thanks because *God is*—and we are alive and the world is beautiful.

It is a warm, sunny day and I am sitting on my patio looking out into the forest of trees, shrubs, and flowers that is Maplelot. (That is what we call our city lot that we planted full of maples.)

I see the red streak of a cardinal sweep low, a flash of crimson against the green hedges. Over in the corner, sitting on a branch of a silver maple, are two fat robins keeping their eyes on several rascally bluejays who are bullying and blustering with their loud squawks.

Two squirrels are playing and frisking up and down a tree, now coming down backward, swishing their tails as they slyly eye the crook of the branch where my husband, Ed, hides pecans and walnuts for them.

Near the fragrant honeysuckle on the fence a circle of bees buzz about as a hummingbird hovers near, ready to move in for a sip of nectar.

And high on a wire in the alley, lording over all, is the mockingbird with its song so sweet it pierces the soul.

Then I think of how the Bible tells us the seraphim sing around the throne of God, "Holy, holy, holy, is the LORD of hosts: the whole earth is full of his glory" (Isa. 6:3).

And I know what they mean.

RESOURCES

The resources in this chapter are as important as any in this book. And if you will use them and absorb them into your mind, the benefits will be astounding.

For praise and thanksgiving opens the mind and the heart in a new way. No matter what the problem, no matter how serious the situation, it is a direct line to God and his mercy and love.

Reading and rereading the "praise psalms" at the end of these resources will prove to you that God lives in the praises of his people.

WE ARE TOLD TO

Give thanks in all circumstances,

for this is God's will for you in Christ Jesus. (I Thess. 5:18, NIV)

AND WE FIND WE ARE

Speaking to ourselves in psalms and hymns and spiritual songs, singing and making melody in our hearts to the Lord;

Giving thanks always for all things unto God and the Father in the name of our Lord Jesus Christ. (Eph. 5:19–20)

SO

Do not be anxious about anything, but in everything, by prayer and petition, with thanksgiving, present your requests to God. (Phil. 4:6, NIV)

AND WE CAN SAY

Great is the LORD, and greatly to be praised; and his greatness is unsearchable.

One generation shall praise thy works to another, and shall declare thy mighty acts. (Ps. 145:3–4)

FOR

From the rising of the sun unto the going down of the same the LORD's name is to be praised. (Ps. 113:3)

AND

I will sing unto the LORD as long as I live: I will sing praise to my God while I have my being.

My meditation of him shall be sweet; I will be glad in the LORD. (Ps. 104:33–34)

My soul shall be satisfied as with marrow and fatness; and my mouth shall praise thee with joyful lips. (Ps. 63:5)

AND FURTHERMORE

In God I will praise his word, in God I have put my trust. (Ps. 56:4)

I will give thee thanks in the great congregation:
I will praise thee among much people. (Ps. 35:18)

I will declare thy name unto my brethren;
In the midst of the congregation will I praise thee. (Ps. 22:22)

Let the heaven and earth praise him, the seas, and every thing that moveth therein. (Ps. 69:34)

SO

O come, let us sing unto the LORD: let us make a joyful noise to the rock of our salvation.
Let us come before his presence with thanksgiving, and make a joyful noise unto him with psalms. (Ps. 95:1–2)

AND

By him therefore let us offer the sacrifice of praise to God continually, that is, the fruit of our lips, giving thanks to his name. (Heb. 13:15)

AND SO WE OFFER THESE PRAISES

O LORD our Lord, how excellent is thy name in all the earth! (Ps. 8:1)

I will praise thee, O LORD, with my whole heart; I will show forth all thy marvelous works. I will be glad and rejoice in thee: I will sing praise to thy name, O thou Most High. (Ps. 9:1–2)

I will sing unto the LORD, because he hath dealt bountifully with me. (Ps. 13:6)

I will praise the LORD according to his righteousness: and will sing praise to the name of the LORD most high. (Ps. 7:17)

I will bless the LORD, who hath given me counsel. (Ps. 16:7)

I will love thee, O LORD, my strength. The LORD is my rock, and my fortress, and my deliverer; my God, my strength, in whom I will trust. (Ps. 18:1–2)

The heavens declare the glory of God; and the firmament showeth his handiwork. (Ps. 19:1)

The earth is the LORD's, and the fulness thereof; the world, and they that dwell therein. (Ps. 24:1)

Unto thee, O LORD, do I lift up my soul. (Ps. 25:1)

The LORD is my light and my salvation; whom shall I fear? The LORD is the strength of my life; of whom shall I be afraid? (Ps. 27:1)

Give unto the LORD, O ye mighty, give unto the LORD glory and strength. Give unto the LORD the glory due unto his name; worship the LORD in the beauty of holiness. (Ps. 29:1–2)

In thee, O LORD, do I put my trust; let me never be ashamed: deliver me in thy righteousness. (Ps. 31:1)

Rejoice in the LORD, O ye righteous: for praise is comely for the upright. Praise the LORD with harp: sing unto him with the psaltery and an instrument of ten strings. Sing unto him a new song; play skilfully with a loud noise. For the word of the LORD is right; and all his works are done in truth. He loveth righteousness and judgment: the earth is full of the goodness of the LORD. (Ps. 33:1–5)

I will bless the LORD at all times: his praise shall continually be in my mouth. (Ps. 34:1)

Let the LORD be magnified, which hath pleasure in the prosperity of his servant. (Ps. 35:27)

As the hart panteth after the water brooks, so panteth my soul after thee, O God. (Ps. 42:1)

Clap your hands, all ye people; shout unto God with the voice of triumph. (Ps. 47:1)

Bless the LORD, O my soul: and all that is within me, bless his holy name. (Ps. 103:1)

Praise ye the LORD. Blessed is the man that feareth the LORD, that delighteth greatly in his commandments. (Ps. 112:1)

Praise ye the LORD from the heavens: praise him in the heights. Praise ye him, all his angels: praise ye him, all his hosts. Praise ye him, sun and moon: praise him, all ye stars of light. Praise him, ye heavens of heavens, and ye waters that be above the heavens. Let them praise the name of the LORD: for he commanded, and they were created. (Ps. 148:1–5)

Let every thing that hath breath praise the LORD. Praise ye the Lord. (Ps. 150:6)

7
THE RIGHT COMPASS
The Need for Direction and Guidance

The Right Compass

When my son, Dwight, was in the fifth or sixth grade, he told me he had broken his compass and asked me to buy him a new one. So I went to the store and bought him a fine drafting compass in its own wooden case.

When I gave it to him, I was surprised to see the dismayed look on his face. "Mom," he said. "That's the wrong kind of compass. I don't want to go in circles. I want to know where I am going!"

And isn't that the desire of us all? We don't want to travel in circles. We want to know where we are going.

Help in guidance and direction is part of our inheritance as children of God. It is another benefit of the Kingdom.

As Christian women we know that God's guidance is a shining beacon in every area of our life: our personal life, our home life, marriage, professional life, children, etc. There is not an area of our life that God's guidance and direction does not touch.

Our life has been made up of decisions. In fact, we are where we are, right now, because of decisions we have made in the past. So the wiser our decisions, the better our life. The wiser our guidance, the better our decisions.

So understanding divine guidance brings a better purpose and direction into our lives.

And we are told that all we have to do is ask.

Let's discuss the prayer for guidance and its three parts.

The Prayer for Guidance

LORD, lead me and guide me. (Ps. 31:3)

In all thy ways acknowledge him, and he shall direct thy paths. (Prov. 3:6)

Whenever we have decisions to make that are important in our life and we do not know the direction in which to go, we can lovingly commit ourselves to God's guidance.

We can affirm that God's light and direction are with us.

The prayer for guidance is an "asking" prayer, and like all "asking" prayers the answers come according to our faith.

The prayer for guidance has three parts:

1. Asking
2. Listening for answers
3. Acting on faith

When we understand these three components of guidance, we find that our guidance becomes more positive and we can say with the psalmist, "He will be our guide even unto death" (Ps. 48:14).

1. *Asking*

"Ask, and it shall be given you." (Luke 11:9)

"If ye ask any thing in my name, I will do it." (John 14:14)

"I will instruct thee and teach thee in the way which thou shalt go." (Ps. 32:8)

These Scriptures and many more of our resources in the Bible tell us to ask for direction and guidance and we will receive it.

This is also stressed in many ways in the Bible by the action of God's people from Abraham to Jesus. They all demonstrate guidance answers.

So we can ask, in faith, knowing that God is our unfailing guide. We will receive what we need. We know the way will be revealed.

The inner light of God—that mind that was in Christ Jesus—will lead us.

Many times we must have patience. Sometimes we must know more about the subject ourselves before we can be guided.

Sometimes there is confusion and cross talk on the line. If we persist and listen with an open and willing mind, we will receive what we need.

2. Listening for Answers

"He who has ears to hear, let him hear." (Matt. 11:15, RSV)

"Listen and hear my voice; pay attention and hear what I say." (Isa. 28:23, NIV)

In most guidance there is a listening time, a time we must quiet our mind and listen for the still, small voice of God within.

To really listen, we must relax and let go, quiet the mind, thought, and emotion of the body. We shut out the clamorings of the outer world and concentrate on the presence of God.

As we replace confusion and uncertainty with the peace of God, we feel it sweep over our soul. Then we are enveloped in a loving, knowing presence that fulfills our every need before we ask.

So be renewed and refreshed as you seek and listen for your guidance. Be filled with an inner security and a feeling of well-being. And God's mantle of peace will lead and guide you.

Often children receive pure guidance easily. They have not yet built barriers and facades to hinder the voice of God.

I remember the first time I received guidance as a child. It happened when I was about eight or nine years old and was lost in a cornfield on my father's farm in Kansas.

Although ours was a wheat farm, we also had about forty acres of corn every year. We children loved to play in the cornfields in the late spring and early summer when it was less than knee high. I loved to see the green and silvery patterns as the wind played over the fields.

But we were cautioned to stay out of the cornfield in the summer, because the green corn grew twelve to fourteen feet high in a lush year. It was like a steamy jungle in the midst of the cornfield. A child could see only a few feet and could easily get lost. If you got lost and panicked and ran, you would exhaust yourself easily in a few minutes.

One day I was out playing by myself and I followed a jack-rabbit without thinking and suddenly there I was, lost in the matted jungle that was the cornfield.

No matter which way I turned I saw nothing but foliage and the cornstalks towering over me like green monsters. The greenhouse effect was hot and steamy and so humid that I couldn't get my breath.

The hot summer sun had turned the field into a torrid dungeon. I panicked and began to run, and immediately found I was drenched in sweat, panting for air.

So I stopped. I knew I had to calm down. Just a few weeks earlier a neighbor woman had become lost and panicked and ran until she died of heat exhaustion.

But what was I to do? It was getting more and more difficult to breathe.

I tried to pray, but all I could remember was "Now I lay me down to sleep," and I didn't like that prayer with its "If I die before I wake." I felt God couldn't hear me if I prayed that prayer. There had to be a better prayer.

Why not just ask for what I needed?

So I prayed something simple and direct. "Please, God, get me out of here!"

Then I received the clearest and most definite guidance of my life. Immediately Something was impressing my mind to go in a certain direction. This was not my everyday, logical mind, because I could tell it was telling me to go in another direction. But now I could tell the two voices apart. And the God-voice was so strong—a tug, a deep feeling, a definite impression that left no doubt.

So I followed that inner voice and within minutes I walked out free.

There are many ways a guidance prayer is answered. It can be an impression on the mind, through another person, something we read or hear, through the Bible—even through a dream. It all depends on the circumstance.

Oftentimes if we stop trying so hard and relax, the answer comes. Great inventors, scientists, writers, and poets have all told stories of fighting for days for solutions. Then they go to bed one night, giving up.

And they awake the next morning with the answer. When they released, it allowed a Greater Guidance to come through with answers.

"Call unto me, and I will answer thee, and show thee great and mighty things, which thou knowest not." (Jer. 33:3)

3. *Acting on Faith*

"If you are willing and obedient, you shall eat the good of the land." (Isa. 1:19, RSV)

"I fear no evil; for thou art with me." (Ps. 23:4, RSV)

"But it is the spirit in a man, the breath of the Almighty, that gives him understanding." (Job 32:8, NIV)

We have learned that the inner spiritual world is built on faith and trust. Guidance prayer is no exception. When we are given answers through guidance we must be willing to follow.

Often this means stepping out on faith, and sometimes into paths that are unknown.

Many times when I receive my guidance it is a step at a time. When I take that first step, I receive the guidance for the next step. But, here again, it means placing our reliance on God.

When we have the courage to follow divine direction and our indwelling Christ, we know our path will be made clear and straight.

"Christ shall give you light." (Eph. 5:14, RSV)

God's Part and Our Part in Guidance

I find that what they say about luck also is true of guidance. "The harder I work, the luckier I get!"

In guidance I find the harder I work, the better I prepare myself, the easier comes my guidance.

For in guidance we have a part and God has a part. Unless we do our part, it is often difficult to find direction from the inner self. For direction often comes *after* we have done preparation or taken a step.

Doing our part is to learn all about the subject for which we need guidance. Then we can ask. If we ask before we learn about the subject, we usually cannot even recognize our guidance, or if we do, we must follow blindly.

I have a friend who wanted to go into business and open up a tearoom. All she had was the idea. She had not done any research or learned any facts about a tearoom. But she expected to receive guidance. Nothing came. All she received from her prayers was a blank.

Then she began to learn about her subject, researching figures and facts. The more she learned, the more new ideas came to her.

These ideas surprised her, for she didn't know where they came from.

The time came when she felt that she had all the information she needed. She asked for guidance and was given a definite impression that the answer was "No!" It was so loud and clear that she couldn't mistake it. But her conscious mind still wanted the tearoom, so she went over her facts with an expert in the field. She was told that she was undercapitalized, the location was not right, and the rent was too high. It confirmed her guidance exactly.

Trouble on the Line

If we had perfect guidance, we all would have the correct answers to all our problems. But it doesn't work that way. We live in a world where we have much static, cross talk, and heaven-knows-what type of interference.

There are two areas where we can help ourselves and keep our guidance clearer.

1. *Our Ideas and Prejudices Set in Stone*

If we had a perfectly open mind, our guidance would be clearer. But it is filtered through our preconceived ideas, "mistaken certainties," and rigid beliefs that aren't necessarily true. Often this holds us back because they are set in the firm concrete of our mind.

One way you can recognize some of these stone pillars in your life is by watching your phrases such as "all the time," "everyone," "no good," and "always." These blanket statements and iron opinions can be everything from ethnic slurs to old wives' tales and "my mother told me's" to "it must be so's."

Each one of us carries a basket of these around. When we look in our basket and clean it out, open our mind, and don't clump people or situations as "always" and "forever," a change comes into our life.

I heard the following illustration many years ago, so it must have been around a long time. It illustrates perfectly how we can be programmed down through the generations.

A young mother was baking a roast. Instinctively, as she had seen her mother do, she cut off both ends of the meat. Then she put it in the large pan and set it in the oven to cook.

She decided to ask her mother why this was done. Her mother said she didn't know, it had always been done that way—cutting off both ends of the meat.

When the grandmother was asked, she referred them to the great-grandmother, from whom she had learned it.

And when the great-grandmother was asked she laughed. It seemed in her day she didn't have a pan large enough to fit a large roast, so she had to lop off some of the meat from both ends.

And so the custom had passed through to the fourth generation before it was questioned.

Be the questioning one in your generation. Help stop some of the habits, prejudices, and customs that hurt, waste, or keep you from being the free self that God created. You will receive more clear and definite guidance.

2. *Allowing Someone to Make a Law for You*

Another hindrance to having a clear, open line to guidance is allowing someone else to make a law for you in certain areas of your life that takes away your free will.

This is not carried from the past generations but is given to you, right now, to accept or reject.

If you accept it, you allow someone else to make a law that can become a truth in your life. And it can supersede or impede anything that comes in through divine guidance.

These "laws" can be anything from a business analyst saying that you cannot get a job because of the high unemployment rate to a doctor giving you a "no chance" prognosis to Madam Sorita down at the Corner Palmistry telling you that you will break a leg next week.

Next time someone tells you something has to be so and it fits into the category of taking your free will away, examine it carefully and don't allow it to be incorporated into your subconscious.

The Joy of a Divine Mandate

What if you have been seeking guidance with patience and persistence and finally the answer comes. Then you are in a wonderful position.

For you are operating under a "divine mandate"—you have broken through and received your guidance with all signs saying, "Go!"

Everything within you is now directed to the completion of your goal. Nothing is more powerful than an idea whose time has come. There is great joy in the person who has the drive and passion to complete a project. There is no conflict in the mind. The decision has been made. There is no division or wavering. Just a single-minded purpose—a thrust-to-goal.

The Bible speaks of such times as "having the single eye." It is a glorious time.

RESOURCES

Guidance is one of the most valuable keys to the Kingdom that enables us to live a better life. Whether our guidance comes as a hunch, an impression, a feeling, an idea, or even something we read or hear, or circumstances, it can bring a better life.

The following resources will help affirm our guidance.

AS WE ASK

LORD, lead me and guide me. (Ps. 31:3)

Show me your ways, O LORD, teach me your paths;
guide me in your truth and teach me. (Ps. 25:4–5, NIV)

AND ALSO WE ASK YOU TO

Send out thy light and thy truth: let them lead me. (Ps. 43:3)

FOR

Thy word is a lamp to my feet and a light to my path. (Ps. 119:105, RSV)

SO

Lead me, O LORD, in your righteousness . . . make straight your way before me. (Ps. 5:8, NIV)

AND
Lead me in the way everlasting. (Ps. 139:24)
SO
Speak, LORD; for thy servant heareth. (I Sam. 3:9)
AND THE LORD GOD SAYS
He that hath ears to hear, let him hear. (Matt. 11:15)

I am the LORD your God, who teaches you what is best for you, who directs you in the way you should go. (Isa. 48:17, NIV)

I lead in the way of righteousness. (Prov. 8:20)
AND FURTHERMORE
I will instruct thee and teach thee in the way which thou shalt go. (Ps. 32:8)

So do not fear, for I am with you; do not be dismayed, for I am your God. I will strengthen you and help you; I will uphold you with my righteous right hand. (Isa. 41:10, NIV)
AND WE REPLY WITH GLADNESS
He restoreth my soul: he leadeth me in the paths of righteousness for his name's sake. (Ps. 23:3)
SO
I will bless the LORD, who hath given me counsel. (Ps. 16:7)

I will praise the LORD, who counsels me; even at night my heart instructs me. (Ps. 16:7, NIV)

For the LORD giveth wisdom: out of his mouth cometh knowledge and understanding. (Prov. 2:6)
AND SO WE SAY
In all thy ways acknowledge him, and he shall direct thy paths. (Prov. 3:6)

8
WHO CARES ABOUT ME?
The Need to Be Loved

✓The Greatest Need

We love, because he first loved us. (I John 4:19, RSV)

By this all men will know that you are my disciples, if you have love for one another. (John 13:35, RSV)

Through the ages people have debated many subjects. There are as many opinions as sands in the seas. But on one subject everyone agrees:

> *Love is the strongest force for good that this planet has ever known.*
> Love is the great cosmic energizer.
> Love is the harmonizing power of the universe.
> For love is All and God is love.
> What is the measure of God's love? Immeasurable.
> What is the depth of his love? Unfathomable.
> How many ways can God's love be expressed? Uncountable.

As Christian women, we know where God's love lives. Within us. For each of us carries the love of God within us without measure. For weren't we created in the image and likeness of God? And God is love.

Yes, we have God's love within us, but with our free will and actions and conditions on earth, it often becomes obscured. Covered up. Buried. But if we really want to express it, we have within us such a lavish love, an overwhelming love, a covering love, so much that we can give enough away to fill the world, the galaxy, the universe—and still have some left over.

For love has a peculiar quality: it is so structured that no matter how much we give away there is always more. Love never goes bankrupt—it is never-ending.

Try it. The minute we give love away, it increases, multiplies, and grows. Throw it about, splash it, spread it, sprinkle it—there is always more.

Love is such a strong radiating force that when we begin to project it outward, it changes our life and the life of others about us.

We also know that the greatest need in our world is for love. So with all that love available, why don't we use it more? Give it more freely to one another? Pass it around? If we used just a small part of the love that is available to us, conflict and strife in the world would end. Wars would cease. The hungry, the poor, the sick, and the unloved would be cared for.

But the adversary had blinded us to the potential of a world of love. And the human ego has played right into the hands of the enemy.

We as Christian women know that love is the answer and are more than willing to do our part. Some of us can only light a match; others can light a candle; and still others, a bright and blinding searchlight of love.

And it all helps to bring God's love into action on earth.

The Love of God Expressed Through Changing People

Be ye transformed by the renewing of your mind. (Rom. 12:2)

Let this mind be in you, which was also in Christ Jesus. (Phil. 2:5)

The ultimate love of God as expressed on earth, was, of course, through Jesus Christ. He came to reconcile us to the Father, to show us the way, to overcome for us, and to teach us to be overcomers. His life, death, and resurrection gave us a new way—the highest spiritual opportunity ever given to anyone on earth. When Jesus left he said he wouldn't leave us comfortless. For he would send us the Holy Spirit, the Comforter, the Helper, to be with us.

92

These are all ways of love. All to help the people on earth. Jesus always helped and healed exactly where the need was. And people's lives changed.

It is no different today. All this great love changes lives. God works a transformation, a renewal, a conversion to change people.

All of us know one or more persons who had an 180-degree turnabout experience. It dazzled to even see it happen, much less experience it. God came into the life, and through his Son, Jesus Christ, did a miracle work of grace. Drunkards never took another drink and fulfilled their potential of love. Criminals became loving and useful citizens, and even the insane became sane. Changes happened in people's lives that could not be disputed.

Probably the first spectacular experience of this type is shown in the story of Saul.

Saul had been the great persecutor of Christians. The Bible says he made "havoc" of the church. He harassed and hurt in every way he could. He threw Christians into prison and was involved in the stoning of Stephen. He had the power to be cruel and he used it.

Then one day on the road to Damascus, Jesus called Saul. The word in today's language would be "zapped!" Wow! There were lights so bright that Saul was blinded for several days. As he lay blinded on the road, he heard Jesus speak to him, and he was changed forever. He became Paul, the zealous worker for Christ who was largely responsible for the spreading of Christianity and the early church.

And it still happens today. There are many Christians with a road-to-Damascus experience. One of the stories of this type of love experience that I will always remember is about a convict named Starr Daily. I heard him speak years ago and what he said stayed with me.

Starr Daily was in prison in solitary confinement. Not only was he a criminal but the prisons didn't know what to do with him, he was so unruly and mean. Those were the days of the "dark holes" and this is where Starr Daily spent most of his time—in the darkness, alone, existing on bread and water. The way the guards, and even his fellow prisoners, expressed it later, there was not one redeeming feature about the man. Everyone had given up on him.

93

Except God.

One day as Starr was lying on the cold cement floor of his pitch-black cell, something happened. There was a light and a warmth about him like he had never experienced before. A warm love flowed over him, infusing him and completely renewing him. At that moment. And he didn't know what or why. But he knew he would never be the same. The love kept pouring through him until it seemed that every cell of his body was vibrant, healthy, and full of love for himself, his fellow human beings, and the world.

He stood up a changed man. Miracles began to happen in his life. Because of the love he suddenly showed and kept showing to his astounding guards, he was taken out of the hole. Soon his love was shining so on everyone with whom he came in contact that they noticed. There wasn't enough he could do to be helpful and kind and loving. Before long the prison doors opened and he went out into the world, lecturing and telling his story about God's love. Through his ministry and books, many lives changed.

Not every Christian comes to God in such a dramatic and awesome way. Probably the majority of us come in what I call "the Peter and Andrew" way, quietly but willingly.

"And he saith unto them, Follow me, and I will make you fishers of men. And they straightway left their nets, and followed him." (Matt. 4:19–20)

When Jesus called Peter and Andrew there was no fanfare. Trumpets didn't blow or lightning flash. They quietly dropped their nets and followed him.

God works differently in everyone's life, but it always adds up to a miracle of love.

The Love of God Expressed on Earth Through Service

For I was hungry and you gave me something to eat,
I was thirsty and you gave me something to drink,
I was a stranger and you invited me in,
I needed clothes and you clothed me,
I was sick and you looked after me,
I was in prison and you came to visit me . . .
I tell you the truth, whatever you did for one of the

94

least of these brothers of mine, you did for me.

(Matt. 25:35–36, 40, NIV)

God expresses himself on earth through our service and love and help for others. Whom else does he have but us? We can help in many ways. We don't have to be a pastor or religious worker to help others. We can help right where we are. And if we are given a particular passion to help in an area of life, so much the better: the needy, the hungry, the lost sheep, the elderly, the sick. Just look about you. You will see something that needs to be done.

When I think of pure service for the love of Christ, I think of Mother Teresa of Calcutta, for she loves as Christ loves. She has dedicated her life to the destitute and dying in an area of the world where the need is desperate.

Mother Teresa says the most prevalent disease today in the world is not of the body, but the feeling of being unwanted, uncared for, unloved, and deserted by everyone. She says she feels the greatest evil in the world is the lack of love, the terrible indifference of people to each other.

Mother Teresa, who was born in Yugoslavia, was twelve years old when she was first called by God. She knew she was going to work with the poor, but it wasn't until she was a nun and made a special retreat that she was called to work in the slums of Calcutta.

She has never had one moment of regret or unhappiness, for her whole life is dedicated to show love to all people. She has been able to show the neglected, many of them are the dying she picks up in the gutters, that they are not forgotten or unloved. The conditions are so adverse that our human mind can't even conceive of them. The dying, the old, the children, the sick, the poor. There is so much to be done.

To Mother Teresa the people she helps are Christ. She sees the Lord in every face and she believes the road to God is through helping our fellow human beings.

The Grace of God as Expressed on Earth

For by grace are ye saved through faith; and that not of yourselves: it is the gift of God. (Eph. 2:8)

How wonderful, in this chapter on love, to be able to write

about my favorite subject of all subjects—grace.

I think it is important that we Christian women thoroughly understand grace, and why it makes Christianity different from any other religion on earth.

For grace goes even beyond our ability to understand love.

Grace is the revolutionary concept that Jesus Christ brought to this world. Grace is God reaching down to humankind. Loving, saving, helping. Grace is always completely in our favor, a one-way gift of pure love from God to us. We don't have to do anything to deserve it, just believe and accept the free gift of love.

Grace is:

> Your Father loves you. (John 15:9)
> Thy sins are forgiven thee. (John 1:29)
> There is no condemnation in Christ Jesus. (Rom. 8:1)
> Love is the perfect law of liberty. (James 1:25)

To really understand grace, let's contrast it with the law, which came before grace, and karma, which is the opposite of grace.

1. *Law*

"For the law was given by Moses, but grace and truth came by Jesus Christ." (John 1:17)

Before Jesus came the law and sacrifice was necessary as shown in the Old Testament. Jesus came and his life and death fulfilled the law and brought grace.

The difference between law and grace is:

The law condemns—Grace redeems.
The law curses—Grace blesses.
The law slays—Grace saves.
The law says *Pay!*—Grace says *It is paid!*
The law says death—Grace says life.
The law says pay for sin—Grace atones.
The law is written on stone—Grace is written in our hearts.
The law means bondage—Grace is freedom for humankind.
The law is fear—Grace is peace.
The law is sacrifice—Grace paid the price.

2. *Karma*

"Ye shall know the truth, and the truth shall make you free." (John 8:32)

"If the Son therefore shall make you free, ye shall be free indeed." (John 8:36)

Where we find the Jewish and Moslem religions caught up in the legalism of the law, we find the Eastern religions tightly bound in karma.

And the opposite of karma is grace.

Karma is the belief in the law of cause and effect carried over to other lifetimes, where one must keep attempting to atone for sins—lifetime after dreary lifetime. Always working to make the good karma outweigh the bad. India, with its hordes of poor suffering people, is a good example of the hopelessness of the people caught on the wheel of karma—people desperately trying to save themselves by making themselves perfect by struggling in the sloughs of the physical dimensions. If they only knew of the pure and holy dimension of the Holy Spirit!

Karma keeps you working at your salvation, carrying your sins. Grace paid the price. You are free. Here and now. There is no hangover. Jesus came and set us free once and for all. Through asking for forgiveness and believing, your past is wiped out.

So grace is love to the uttermost heights.

The Prayer of Pure Love

There is something we can add to our prayers to make them more effective—love in its purest form.

I believe a prayer said with the attitude of pure love is the most powerful prayer on earth. No matter what type of prayer we pray—asking, praise, thanksgiving, etc.—when it is done with pure love in our heart, it turns into a miracle prayer. For there is nothing that love cannot conquer.

Love is your secret weapon. You don't have to let anyone know what you are doing, for the results from a prayer of love will show first of all in you, and then in the condition or people about you.

The following are a few examples of the prayer of love. Of course it can be used in more ways, in fact, in every way in your life.

1. *The Prayer of Pure Love for Peace and Harmony About You*

All of us at one time or another find ourselves in an atmosphere of turbulence and strife, where frustrations, fretfulness, and irritation seem to overwhelm us.

The prayer of pure love can bring peace.

A friend of mine, Mary Lou, had a nearly intolerable situation in her office. It was continuing day after day. The company was in financial turmoil, the people were all at odds with one another, even the mailboy was so cantankerous that he had the switchboard operator and the file clerks always crying.

One day Mary Lou decided that this had gone on long enough. Immediately she began praying that the love of God was in this place. And where the love of God is, peace and harmony reign. She affirmed this over and over while showing extra attention and kindness to those who were most agitated.

Mary Lou realized that she had to affirm from a center of peace and stability within herself, so in the evenings she would work with her Bible and verses on peace and harmony such as:

"Thou wilt keep him in perfect peace, whose mind is stayed on thee." (Isa. 26:3)

"And the peace of God, which passeth all understanding, shall keep your hearts and minds through Christ Jesus." (Phil. 4:7)

"He maketh the storm a calm." (Ps. 107:29)

"Be still, and know that I am God." (Ps. 46:10)

And the next day she would go to work praying with a deep love for her company and the employees. She loved her company in a special way. She appreciated her job, and everyone had been good to her so she could pray with pure love for their welfare. As she went about her daily business she visualized God's love "covering" each worker, from the president of the company to the warehouse helpers. She began to see harmony and peace in that place NOW. Then she began silently to praise and give thanks because it was so.

The situation did change—not all at once, but little by little. But the glorious thing was that Mary Lou, while yet in the midst of the storm, had a peace and tranquillity about her that she said had to be a pure gift from God. For she was now operating from a pure center of calm no matter what was going on about her.

Love was the answer.

2. *The Prayer of Pure Love for Reconciliation*

"He that loveth another hath fulfilled the law."(Rom. 13:8)

One time I was teaching a class on prayer, and we decided to pray the prayer of pure and absolute love, as much as is humanly possible. To make it even more difficult, we chose to pray with love for those from whom we were estranged. These were mostly family members, a runaway child, an errant husband, sisters, brothers, etc.

Now when you pray the prayer of absolute and pure love, you make no judgments, no conditions—just see the person you are praying for in perfect love.

That means you put aside everything you know about the person. And everything that happened between you—all the hurts, the disappointments, disillusionments, unkindnesses—whatever. You see only God, you think only of God, and you feel only God. We wanted to be able to love one another as Jesus loved.

We didn't even attempt to pray for others in this way for the first few meetings, for we knew we had to pray for ourselves, asking forgiveness and cleansing ourselves of negatives. To pray in complete love and hold no rancor for someone who had hurt us or had been unkind to us (to say the least, for some had horror stories to tell) would give our spiritual muscles a good workout. But we all had a deep desire and determination for reconciliation. And we believed in the power of prayer.

After we had prayed for cleansing and felt that we had come to the point where we could pray for the person in true Christlike love (as much as was humanly possible for us), we began. We held the person up in love—true love with no conditions.

During the week we carried a card with the person's name on it which we took out several times a day, visually looking at the name in forgiveness and love. We would pray and affirm God's love somewhat in this manner, for each of us had a different prayer to suit the need.

> God's love surrounds you and me, now. God's love is projected from me to you. God's love through me reaches you, dissolving anything that is not like Christ. I ask that God's love through me, brings complete forgiveness. God's love is working harmony in our

lives now. God loves you unconditionally. I love you unconditionally.

In the love and the name of Jesus Christ we are both free in love, *now*.

By the end of this six-week class many changes occurred. First, everyone reported a change in their own way of seeing others. They felt that they had more compassion and love and patience with people. Several were reunited with members of their family: an errant husband returned to ask forgiveness and with the willingness to begin again and a runaway daughter called home on the runaway hotline. (She later returned home.)

One of the stories I remember most vividly was of Wendy. Wendy had much sorrow about her relationship with her sister, Babs. Babs had seemed to have been born with a grudge against her family and had not only estranged herself from them, but had done many cruel and unloving things.

Wendy spent most of the six-week period convincing herself that it was possible for a reconciliation. She had to overcome unbelief, then work with forgiveness and love, and then see Babs surrounded with love.

During the last week of our meeting, Babs called Wendy. Out of the blue. She didn't want anything but just to see how Wendy was. Something she had never done before. And she was kind and courteous and caring. It was a beautiful beginning that eventually led to a full reconciliation.

The prayer of pure love can work miracles.

3. *The Prayer of Pure Love Always Wishes Others Well*

There is a special prayer of love that always wishes others well. It negates even the subtle undermining of jealousy and envy that catches us unaware.

For wasn't it jealousy and envy that caused Cain to slay Abel? And the mark of Cain has been carried down through the generations and can catch us in its snare.

Usually what catches us is when we see inequity all about us. Someone has more or has done better, so we think, What about us? This throws us into the negative and makes the situation even worse. For now we are in worse condition than before, for we have lost our resources.

So our only chance is to give praise for where we are at this moment, as Christian women, and for what we have and to build from there using Christian principles.

Pure love releases us from the negatives of jealousy and envy. I wrote the following affirming prayer of love that will help any situations that are tinged with the mark of Cain.

> I look at others about me through the eyes of love. I wish others well in their endeavors. I wish them success and love.
>
> And what God has done for others, he will do for me. In a way that is right for me. And as I believe and work, my good will come to me. I give thanks for this and listen with open ears and mind for guidance and direction.
>
> I am filled with the love of God. And I give thanks for the goodness that comes to me.
>
> "For the LORD is good; his mercy is everlasting; and his truth endureth to all generations." (Ps. 100:5)

RESOURCES

The love resources are as powerful as any you will find, for they help bring God's love into your life, undergirding everything you do.

You can use them separately or with other resources. They always strengthen anything they touch. And Love always heals, comforts, and uplifts.

WE BEGIN WITH THE TWO GREAT COMMANDMENTS THAT JESUS BROUGHT

Thou shalt love the Lord thy God with all thy heart,
and with all thy soul, and with all thy strength,
and with all thy mind; and thy neighbor as thyself. (Luke 10:27)

This is my commandment, That ye love one another, as I have loved you. (John 15:12)

As the Father hath loved me, so have I loved you: continue ye in my love.

If ye keep my commandments, ye shall abide in my love. (John 15:9–10)

SO

Love one another. (John 15:17)

FOR

By this shall all men know that ye are my disciples, if ye have love one to another. (John 13:35)

AND WE KNOW

He that loveth not knoweth not God; for God is love. (I John 4:8)

AND

There is no fear in love; but perfect love casteth out fear. (I John 4:18)

AND WE CAN SAY

We love him, because he first loved us. (I John 4:19)

SO

I will love thee, O LORD, my strength. (Ps. 18:1)

For God so loved the world, that he gave his only begotten Son, that whosoever believeth in him should not perish, but have everlasting life. (John 3:16)

AND WE ARE TOLD

That Christ may dwell in your hearts by faith;
that ye, being rooted and grounded in love . . . (Eph. 3:17)

WILL

Know the love of Christ, which passeth knowledge, that ye might be filled with all the fulness of God. (Eph. 3:19)

SO

Beloved, if God loved us so [very much], we also ought to love one another. (I John 4:11, AMP)

And walk in love—esteeming and delighting in one another— as Christ loved us. (Eph. 5:2, AMP)

AND WE ARE TOLD NO MATTER WHAT THE CONDITIONS

The God of love and peace shall be with you. (II Cor. 13:11)

To show forth thy loving-kindness in the morning, and thy faithfulness every night. (Ps. 92:2)

So rich is He in His mercy! Because of and in order to satisfy the great and wonderful and intense love with which He loved us. (Eph. 2:4, AMP)

SO WE SAY

I will love thee, O LORD, my strength. (Ps. 18:1)

AND HE REPLIES

I love them that love me; and those that seek me early shall find me. (Prov. 8:17)

Yea, I have loved thee with an everlasting love:
therefore with loving-kindness have I drawn thee. (Jer. 31:3)

SO WE CAN SAY WITH CERTAINTY

Nor height, nor depth, nor any other creature, shall be able to separate us from the love of God, which is in Christ Jesus our Lord. (Rom. 8:39)

SO SINCE

Love never fails. (I Cor. 13:8, NIV)

Follow the way of love. (I Cor. 14:1, NIV)

FOR

Faith, hope, love abide, these three;
but *the greatest of these is love.* (I Cor. 13:13, RSV; italics added)

9
JOINED TOGETHER IN MARRIAGE
The Need for Companionship

Marriage—A Walk in Love

A time to love. (Eccl. 3:8)

In the previous chapter I discussed many ways of love.
But there are more.

There is marriage—a very special gift of love from God.

I like to think of marriage as a union of love between a man and
a woman that is a circle. They meet in tenderness, love, and
devotion and become one. That completes the circle and expression of love from which they originated.

When two people meet and fall in love a special chemistry
happens. Writers and poets have tried for centuries to explain
this miracle with words.

But even the most beautiful words have difficulty doing justice
to the specialness of love—and marriage.

I like the way Solomon expresses it in the Song of Songs. This
book of the Bible was written as a type of play, and Solomon has
the woman say these words to her lover:

> "Place me like a seal over your heart,
>   like a seal over your arm;
> for love is as strong as death,
>   its jealousy unyielding as Sheol.
> It burns like blazing fire,
>   like a mighty flame.
> Many waters cannot quench love:

rivers cannot wash it away.
. . . .
Come away, my lover,
    and be like a gazelle
or like a young stag
    on the spice-laden mountains."
    (Song of Songs 8:6–7, 14, NIV)

Marriage in Bible Times

What was marriage like in Bible times?

When we read the Bible, especially the Old Testament, we find many stories of people and marriage, some loving and faithful, others not honest to their spouse—or themselves. There were those who were caring, others who caused much suffering, and still others who murdered for love.

It sounds quite modern, doesn't it?

Let's take the story of David for an example. Of all the people in the Old Testament, we know that David was God's man. He is called a "man after God's own heart" and also spoken of as "beloved of God."

Yet David broke the law of love with Bathsheba. He knew she was married but he had an affair with her. Not only that, he wanted her so badly that he sent her husband, Uriah, into the front of the battle so that he would be killed—a sort of murder by remote control. When Uriah was killed, David married Bathsheba, who was already pregnant. That baby died, but the next baby would be the great King Solomon.

There was no doubt about it, David was human and sinned. But he also had a contrite heart and asked for forgiveness of God. And later that was the same great King David, who wrote the psalms, the greatest devotions to God ever written.

Let's continue our story wth David and Bathsheba's son, the great and wise king, Solomon. In those days very often your wealth was judged by how many wives you had. King Solomon was rich enough to have over one thousand wives. That surely would be enough to give any man a headache, but it gave him great admiration and social status in the community.

Now the New Testament doesn't tell us about many marriages. We know of the marriage of Mary and Joseph and their close love for each other and their Special Child. And a little bit about several other marriages, but really nothing personal as is given in the Old Testament. But it doesn't really matter. For Jesus gives us some instructions and then his laws of love apply to marriage as they do to any other human endeavor.

Although customs are different today (thank goodness, one wife per husband), yet in reading the Bible we find that basically people haven't changed that much. Social structures have changed and we have added unbelievable technology, but the human desires are still the same. The need to love and be loved by that special person.

The Interdependence and Freedom of Man and Woman

It is important that we as Christian women understand the interdependence of man and woman as shown in the Bible. And the freedom.

It begins like this:

"The LORD God said, 'It is not good for the man to be alone. I will make a helper suitable for him' " (Gen. 2:18, NIV).

And then we are told that God looked about him and couldn't find a suitable helper, so he made a woman for the man from the man's ribs (literally the text says from a part of the man's side).

So then the man could say:

> "This is now bone of my bones
> and flesh of my flesh;
> she shall be called 'woman'
> for she was taken out of man."
> (Gen. 2:23, NIV)

So this established a MAN-woman interdependence and we are told:

"For this reason a man will leave his father and mother and be united to his wife, and they will become one flesh." (Gen. 2:24, NIV)

It is emphasized in this way in the New Testament:

"Even so husbands should love their wives as [being in a sense] their own bodies. He who loves his own wife loves himself.

"For no man ever hated his own flesh, but nourishes and

carefully protects and cherishes it, as Christ does the church."
(Eph. 5:28–29, AMP)

And marriage is continually compared to the church. As the husband is head of the wife so is Christ head of the church.

"Husbands, love your wives, as Christ loved the church."
(Eph. 5:25, RSV)

Now that we have seen the MAN-woman interdependence, let's see the WOMAN-man interdependence.

"For although the first woman came out of man,
all men have been born from women ever since,
and both men and women came from God their Creator."

(I Cor. 11:12, TLB)

Not only is there this special intertwined relationship between man and woman (when compared to the church it is all spoken of as a "mystery"), but Christ came to bring freedom to both sexes. He restored woman to a responsible partnership with man as part of God's redeeming process in the world.

Here is the spiritual emancipation proclamation for both men and women:

"There is neither Jew nor Greek, slave nor free, MALE NOR FEMALE, for you are all one in Christ Jesus." (Gal. 3:28, NIV; emphasis added)

"It is for freedom that Christ has set us free. Stand firm, then, and do not let yourselves be burdened again by a yoke of slavery." (Gal. 5:1, NIV)

"Where the Spirit of the Lord is, there is freedom." (II Cor. 3:17, NIV)

We find that Jesus always dealt directly on a one-to-one basis with women in the Bible. He forgave sins freely, healed the sick women or their children, and was always understanding and loving.

When Jesus visited the house of Mary and Martha he commended Mary for sitting at his feet and learning directly from him. It wasn't that what Martha was doing was not important, but Jesus in another way was telling us that in seeking first the Kingdom all things then will be added. In other words, get your spiritual resources in proper perspective then everything else will fall into place. Mary had an opportunity to sit at the feet of the Master and she took it.

Marriage—and Divorce

Before we go any farther into the chapter on marriage, let's give comfort to the bruised.

We know that today a strain is put on marriage as never before. Nearly one out of every two marriages fails or is in severe trouble.

So we Christian women must use our resources in a way as we never have before to keep equilibrium in our lives. Sometimes, no matter what is done to help the marriage, it ends in divorce. Even among believers. The situation becomes so unhappy and confused that the marriage is torn into a million pieces.

No matter what the reason for the divorce—or whose fault or no one's fault—there are no winners. For divorce always leaves the bruised and the wounded. There are hurts and scars and also a grieving time for the death of even the most miserable of marriages.

My friend Alicia has just gone through a shocking and unhappy time. Her divorce was not of her choosing. One day her husband announced he wanted to be free. Nothing could change his mind and so he walked out of her life.

Of course Alicia's world was shattered. Not only had she lost her love but her home and everything they had worked for. And her dreams and goals. Alicia felt betrayed, unloved, and emotionally bereft.

But Alicia was fortunate that she had her resources. But even at that it was difficult at first. She had to begin all over again. She had to make a new life. And she had times when she wondered where God was. Had he deserted her? But then she would realize that God was with her and would comfort her if she allowed him to.

So step-by-step Alicia found her way back. As I talked with her through those times, I could feel a greater strength grow within her, for Alicia was now "standing tall" inside.

As the love of God and her resources sustained her, she found strength she didn't know she had. Even her talents had been sharpened and honed fine. For from what could have been weak and self-pitying times came some of her greatest work as a writer.

For Alicia found, as we all do no matter what the challenge, that the love of Christ is greater than the problem. There is nothing beyond the reach of God's forgiving and restoring love. Wounds can be healed and new beginnings and goals are ahead.

What Makes Marriage Work?

What are the ingredients that make a marriage work? What does one do to have a marriage that is loving, caring, and fulfilling to both partners? What *is* the secret?

Good questions! Is there a sage somewhere who has the answers? But who would be presumptuous enough to think they knew anyway?

So I will just talk about my experience. Edward and I were married when I was eighteen (he was twenty-three) and we have been married more than thirty-five years. We have two children, Dwight and Renée.

We have had our mountaintops and valleys—like every married couple. But mostly there was and is love. And caring. And sharing. That helped us over the rough spots.

As I look back through the years there are some basics that stand out—not only in our marriage but in the marriages of friends and others about us. I have condensed them down to four categories: love, commitment, communication, and caring.

1. *Love*

What more can be said about love? Hasn't it all been said by someone sometime? Of course, but let me tell you my ideas. I have found that marriage love has three parts, which are all spoken of in the Bible: *eros* (sexual), *philio* (friendship), and *agape* (Christlike) love.

They are all components of the love of marriage. Sometimes one, other times two, or still other times all three are in operation at one time.

Eros—sexual love
"And they shall be one flesh." (Gen. 2:24)

This is the love union that makes marriage special. Without a strong sexual love (unless unusual circumstances) a marriage has difficulty surviving. This is the fulfillment, the pleasure, the ultimate way a man and a woman can express married love.

Philio—friendship

"A friend loveth at all times." (Prov. 17:17)

What a delight to find that your marriage partner is also your best friend! I believe that this should be the goal of the marriage partners—to establish such a relationship that you are friends. Someone you can talk with, tell your troubles to, who will listen, comfort, and help. And you return the friendship.

Agape—Christlike love

"As the Father hath loved me, so have I loved you: continue ye in my love." (John 15:9)

This is the deepest and most caring love possible. This is the love that goes the extra mile, and there are many extra miles in marriage. This is the love that gives without expecting something in return, and marriage is full of such moments.

Agape brings the highest of spiritual love into the marriage, but it also brings in something else: strong, definite, and positive prayer power.

Remember the Scripture that says:

"If two of you shall agree on earth as touching any thing that they shall ask, it shall be done for them of my Father which is in heaven.

"For where two or three are gathered together in my name, there am I in the midst of them." (Matt. 18:19–20)

This is a powerful promise of Jesus. Notice the qualification: "two gathered together." Well, a marriage is two people.

The power and strength that comes from marriage partners holding hands and praying together can shake the world. There is a specialness and a loving peace that can be found no other way.

What better prayer partner to have than your marriage partner? Two people with a common interest.

2. Commitment

Marriage is a deep and abiding commitment of love between two people, legalized by the state and sanctified and blessed by God.

It is a commitment not to be taken lightly. If we lose sight of the original premise of marriage—two who have become one—and forget the goals of keeping this marriage intact, the partnership can run into trouble.

All the energy of the couple should be focused and have as its ultimate goal the preserving of the marriage as it grows in love. If this is forgotten, the adversary can creep in and make the marriage turn on itself in enmity.

So everything that happens in a marriage should be filtered through a screen that says:

"This is a marriage-in-love, blessed by God that is happening here."

Several years ago a survey was made of fourteen hundred marriages. One half ended in divorce and the other half survived.

When the problems of the marriages of both groups were analyzed, there was no difference. The challenges were the same. The only difference was that the couples who stayed married tried harder. Rather than giving up, both partners looked for solutions and gave all their attention to the goal of preserving the marriage.

Your Christian resources will probably get a greater workout in marriage (and in relationships with your children) than in any other area of your life. So stay close to your resources.

It always amazes me the time and effort and money that people spend on weddings. Then more is spent on furnishing an apartment or a house and on cars. Yet when the marriage runs into trouble no effort is made to get help. It is left to sag and wither and die.

Edward and I have always had a saying in our marriage if it suddenly became rough and bumpy: "Our marriage is getting off the track." That meant something was wrong, bad habits, no communication, dull or boring times were creeping in—any of a number of problems. And we knew the marriage needed a spark, help, anything to keep it from slipping off the track. It was like a train in danger of being derailed.

Then we had to make changes, do what was necessary to get the marriage back to being vibrant, viable, running smoothly down the track.

To keep a marriage from floundering, you must be committed to that marriage.

The conflict-competition syndrome is one that I see too often in marriages today. The commitment on the surface seems intact, but underneath it is a seething caldron. It is as if the marriage had a continual low-grade fever that was sapping its strength, for the partners have become enemies, each pulling in a different direction.

The terrible thing about this pattern is that it can become the "fashionable" way to fight. I have seen committed believers, even pastors and their wives, play this game. They have gone underground in a war of wills.

Della's story is typical. Tom and Della are two very bright but stubborn young people. They both hold down responsible positions and are taught to be competitive, reach for the top, win at all costs—become number one.

And they have brought this type of thinking home into their marriage partnership. Win. Win. Win. Even in the little things.

So they sabotage each other—anything to frustrate each other. There are a thousand ways to be mean, and before long they know them all. And they win battles but eventually both end up losing the war.

Della asks: "How do we break out of this syndrome? How do I get my marriage back to a true partnership with common goals?"

It isn't easy because two strong egos are involved, but it can be done. And it is so much easier if you have the cooperation of your partner. You can sit down in a conference and both recognize that a marriage is made up of the energy of its partners, just like any business, company, or corporation. And unless this energy is harnessed, disciplined, and dedicated toward the cooperation of the marriage, the marriage can destroy itself. So why continue being enemies and make yourself miserable and your marriage sick?

If you don't have the cooperation of your partner, you can still break the impasse. It is a humbling experience, for you must practice nonresistance, stop retaliation, and double the love. Add extra praise and understanding and kindness. Show your partner that you are not in a game of wills any longer. Make every action one of cooperation—not competition. The resources of Chapter 8 on love, Chapter 6 on praise, and Chapter 14 on forgiveness are especially helpful.

3. *Communication*

We are told that the number one problem in marriage is lack of communication.

When there is open dialogue, true communication between two willing people, any problem can be worked out.

True communication is not only talking but *listening*—really trying to understand what the partner is saying.

Listening in a caring way is one of the greatest gifts you can give your marriage partner. Listening in a way that you can say you know him as if you had "walked in his moccasins."

One time I was doing research on marriages that had lasted fifty or more years for a planned book. I found one thread that ran through all the marriages.

"We talk to each other but lightly, with a sense of humor."

One man, married fifty-three years, summed it up this way: "I guess you would say it's making an extra effort to be 'companionable'!"

To make a marriage more "companionable" and help communication I like what I call the Me-You-Us Technique.

Once or twice a year (oftener if necessary) each partner sits down with three sheets of paper, entitled "Me," "You," and "Us." And they write down what they want from the marriage and what they are willing to give. For instance:

> ME: What do I desire from my marriage at this point? What are my short-term goals? Long-term goals? What changes do I see that I could make to make the marriage better? What can I do to show more love? To receive more love? What things are bothering me?
>
> YOU: What do I wish for my partner? What do I think my partner needs at this time? How can I make the marriage better for my partner? How can I show more loving and caring to my partner?
>
> US: What do I wish for my marriage? What goals? What do I see that would make the marriage better? How can the energies of the marriage be used more constructively?

You can add more questions according to what is important in your life and marriage now. The important thing is, as you discuss this, to be honest but kind and loving.

4. Caring

Under this category come all the good things that make a marriage a joyful, fulfilling, and tender relationship.

Caring can be something as simple as treating each other with courtesy and good manners, which can bring an immediate change for the better in any marriage.

Or it can be to:

> Support and uplift each other.
> Seize every opportunity to make your partner look good.
> Never dig into the past. Let it be dead.
> Neglect the roast, the President, but never each other.
> Arrange to have strictly private times with each other.
> Never go to bed mad. Rose Kennedy said no matter what she made this a rule. She said going to bed mad was such a waste of time and energy.
> Exercise your ego by looking your partner straight in the eye and admit a mistake and ask for forgiveness.
> Never allow a day to go by without praising and complimenting each other. Be lavish with sincere appreciation.
> Avoid unpleasant conversation. Have weekly times to discuss what is unpleasant to one or both partners, work it out and let it go until the next session.
> Understand and fulfill each other's sexual needs.
> Recognize your mate as a person, with the right to think and feel. Give each other space to grow.
> Never try to change each other. Force won't work. But both of you can change gently through growth and love.
> Never allow your marriage to become dull and stagnant. Stimulate with interesting ideas, books, music, clubs, church, hobbies.

I once heard someone ask Marlo Thomas, who is a strong-willed person in her own right, how she managed to survive with such a strong father as Danny Thomas. Then she turned right around and married a man of even more decided opinions, Phil Donahue. She said, "We are gentle with each other."

So be gentle. It is one of the most beautiful words in the English language for a marriage.

My Necklace of Love

A woman loves:
    as a child
    as a daughter
    as a wife
    as a mother
    as a friend
    as a person

A woman has many love moments. Stories of love that are to be savored and cherished.

So it is good to stop our activity and sit down and review some of the "love times" in our life. What we will do is make ourselves a "necklace of love."

I find that when I put the precious moments on my necklace of love, they don't slip away. They are mine forever.

My necklace of love is at least a triple strand by now, hanging to my knees. I'll pick a jewel from it now, which comes to mind because it is so ridiculously full of love and laughter and we were young and in love.

It was the summer of 1951 and I was pregnant with our first child, Dwight. It was also one of the hottest summers of all time. We had over forty days over 100 degrees and no electric fan or air conditioner. And to compound the problem we had a water shortage, so water was rationed. We could only use water to drink, to cook, and for one bath a week.

We lived in a little house with only a stove, a refrigerator, and a bed. Money was scarce and we had put every extra cent we had toward paying off the doctor and hospital for the coming baby.

Despite the ban on water, I had planted some zinnias and a morning-glory vine near the back door. I kept them alive by carrying out the bath water.

Our son was born on September 3, a day that still holds the record at 105 degrees. And appropriately enough it was Labor Day that year.

The day came when Edward was supposed to come and pick up me and his new son and take us home. He was late but finally he arrived. Since our budget didn't allow for flowers, he had brought some from our yard. It was the scraggliest, scrawniest, dried-up, woebegone bouquet made of our zinnias and morning glories. They drooped and sagged and flopped forlornly.

But they were the most beautiful flowers I had ever seen. I have received rare orchids and velvety roses since then, but nothing will ever be more beautiful than that ragged bouquet, our new son, and the love in my husband's eyes.

When Edward took us home and told me what had happened that morning and why he was so late, the flowers became doubly precious.

It seemed that the hospital had miscalculated and said that we owed another hundred dollars. And they wanted it before I left the hospital. So Edward had spent all morning getting that hundred dollars together to "bail" us out. He robbed the sugar bowl, the bottom of purses in our closet, and borrowed and hocked a few things. Meanwhile the flowers were in the car wilting away in the heat.

Finally, he got the money together. And I was allowed to go home with my red, wrinkled-faced, long-legged son who grew up to be six feet five.

On our thirty-fifth wedding anniversary I wrote Edward the following poem:

TO EDWARD
ON OUR 35TH WEDDING ANNIVERSARY

Where have the years gone?
They have slipped by as jewels,
Each precious, each fulfilling,
Strung on the golden chain of our love.

Thirty-five years ago, young and eager,
We began the first step of our marriage journey.
Our love was new and sparkling
And we thought that was all there was.

But our love increased as we walked together
And began to shine like a special diamond
   of a thousand facets
   as it was polished
Through joys and sorrows, challenges and triumphs,
   Until like vintage wine
   It has become rich and full.

And we found our love could multiply,
For our joy was increased by two—
Dwight and Renée, evidence of our love,
Part of us extended to the future
Keeping our flame alive.

The joys now ahead are precious, it is true,
But they can yet increase,
The goals and dreams do not die—
They are vibrant and alive and there is much ahead.

RESOURCES

These resources can be studied and read with the ones in Chapter 8 on love, if you wish. They also go well and give added help when used with Chapter 6 on praise and Chapter 15 on joy.

IT BEGAN THIS WAY WHEN GOD SAID

It isn't good for man to be alone; I will make a companion for him, a helper suited to his needs. (Gen. 2:18, TLB)

SO GOD MADE A LOVING COMPANION FOR THE MAN AND

This explains why a man leaves his father and mother and is joined to his wife in such a way that the two become one person. (Gen. 2:24, TLB)

AND THEY DID

Love one another. (John 15:17)

AND THEY LEARNED THIS ABOUT LOVE

If I have . . . faith so that I can remove mountains, but have not love [God's love in me]

I am nothing—a useless nobody. (I Cor. 13:2, AMP)

AND

Love is very patient and kind, never jealous or envious, never boastful or proud, never haughty or selfish or rude.

Love does not demand its own way.

It is not irritable or touchy.

It does not hold grudges. (I Cor. 13:4–5, TLB)

FOR

If you love someone you will be loyal to him no matter what the cost. You will always believe in him, always expect the best of him, and always stand your ground in defending him. (I Cor. 13:7, TLB)

FOR

Love goes on forever . . . faith, hope, and love—and the greatest of these is love. (I Cor. 13:8, 13, TLB)

AND

Happy are those who long to be just and good,
for they shall be completely satisfied.
Happy are the kind and merciful,
for they shall be shown mercy.
Happy are those whose hearts are pure,
for they shall see God. (Matt. 5:6–8, TLB)

AND WE KNOW THAT AS YOU LIVE TOGETHER

A joyful heart is good medicine, but a broken spirit dries up the bones. (Prov. 17:22)

AND

A soft answer turneth away wrath: but grievous words stir up anger.
The tongue of the wise useth knowledge aright. (Prov. 15:1–2)

SO

A wise woman builds her house, while a foolish woman tears hers down by her own efforts. (Prov. 14:1, TLB)

AND DID YOU KNOW?

It is better to eat soup with someone you love than steak with someone you hate. (Prov. 15:17, TLB)

ALSO

Gentle words cause life and health; griping brings discouragement. (Prov. 15:4, TLB)

SO REMEMBER

Kind words are like honey—enjoyable and healthful. (Prov. 16:24, TLB)

FOR

A dry crust eaten in peace is better than steak every day along with argument and strife. (Prov. 17:1, TLB)

AND THIS MAKES FOR A HAPPIER MARRIAGE

If you are angry, don't sin by nursing your grudge.
Don't let the sun go down with you still angry—
get over it quickly. (Eph. 4:26–27, TLB)

AND HOW MANY TIMES SHOULD YOU FORGIVE?

I tell you, not up to seven times, but seventy times seven! (Matt. 18:22, AMP)

AND LASTLY

Honor your marriage and its vows, and be pure. (Heb. 13:4, TLB)

FOR

Humility and reverence for the Lord will make you both wise and honored. (Prov. 15:33, TLB)

10
THE TOUGHEST JOB

The Need to Mother and to Nurture

A Child—God's Gift to Us

For unto us a child is born. (Isa. 9:6)

A child is God's special gift to a man and a woman. It is a gift of love that originated in love.

Being a mother to that child, loving it and nurturing it and helping it to grow is one of the most rewarding jobs in the world.

Yet it isn't always easy. Like most things on earth that are worthwhile, it must be worked at with love and patience and persistence.

Since we are all God's children—mother, father, and child—his loving wisdom guides and protects us all.

As you give birth (or adopt), you nurture, guide, teach, and love a new person into this world, thus giving a gift of yourself to the future.

A Mother's Love

I will comfort you there as a little one is comforted by its mother. (Isa. 66:13, TLB)

We have talked of love in its various forms in the preceding two chapters, so now we add another type of love: the special love of a mother for her child or children.

It is so special that God, in trying to explain how much he loves his people, says he will comfort them as a little one is comforted by its mother.

For a mother's love is nurturing, compassionate, and deep. I believe that nothing outside of God's love is greater.

And a Christian mother's love is comforting, sustaining, and always forgiving. Love is a bridge between mother and child—a carrier of strength, courage, and confidence.

My grandmother, Katherine Graf, was the mother of twelve children, eleven living. My father, Alexander Graf, was the next to the oldest of the eleven children. When I was born the youngest uncle and aunt, Victor and Esther, were only three or four years older than I. So there was always a passel of children around.

I remember going to visit my grandmother and seeing her working serenely in what to me, today, would be chaos. She was a quiet woman, not very tall and always busy, for with that many children, how could she ever catch up?

On Sunday we would visit and I would be fascinated with the cooking going on. Cakes would be made in sheets as big as my kitchen table is today. If it was cold weather, Jell-O with fruit in bowls the size of small washtubs would be cooling in the cold back bedrooms. And a ten-pound roast was sizzling away in the big oven. The table was long enough for sixteen people with long benches on either side. Even then, when we ate, we had to eat in two shifts.

And children. Children were everywhere, underfoot, inside, outside, running, playing, talking, screaming. By the time the children, grandchildren, and friends were all together, we had quite a crowd. Yet Grandmother Graf, in the midst of the organized chaos, knew exactly what was going on.

Her secret was simple: she began nearly every sentence with the words, "The Lord and I . . . . " And when she needed something done—and there was always something to do—she would say, "How about the Lord and you and I peeling this batch of potatoes?" Somehow when she made the Lord our partner, it always made the job seem so much more important—and she emphasized this by the tone of her voice.

Soon several of us would be busy peeling the huge sack of potatoes to fry with onions in the large cast-iron skillets.

Another group would be over in a corner chopping onions and

laughing with tears from the onion fumes running down their cheeks. Three giggling girls were setting the table. And still others would be sent down to the cellar to choose vegetables and fruits from the hundreds and hundreds of jars that Grandmother and the older girls had canned.

We worked hard, for Grandmother had a way of making everyone feel important. You were not only working you were "helping" and that made you feel special.

Before long we were lining up for hugs—a hug from Grandmother was a special thank-you for a job well done.

Rearing eleven children who all turned out healthy and hardworking was quite a feat. I am in awe thinking about it. Two children have kept me busy. But looking back at Katherine Graf's life, I can see that one of her great secrets was her phrase "The Lord and I" that she affirmed continually. For she knew that one with God was a majority.

A Mother's Objective

May the Lord richly bless both you and your children. (Ps. 115:14, TLB)

Someone once said, "A mother is not a person to lean on, but a person to make leaning unnecessary."

From the moment of birth a mother's goal should be twofold: give the child the nurturing and training necessary and the proper spiritual disciplines so the child will be able eventually to stand alone.

We do our children an injustice if we attempt to hold them back or restrict them, limit or even attempt to bind them to us. Children must be allowed to mature and learn to stand on their own.

We have our children only for a time—long enough to teach them to leave the nest and fly alone.

Consider the eagle. She builds her nest on high crags and cliffs of mountaintops. When the time comes for the eaglet to fly, the mother pushes it out of the nest or even carries it high into the sky—and lets it fall.

The trip to the ground is long, and during that time the eaglet becomes an eagle. And flies. Or gets smashed.

Of course the human situation is not so abrupt or dangerous, but the time does come when the children leave. We wish them well and send them on to begin their life knowing that God is with them.

Wisdom Is the Principal Thing

Get wisdom, get understanding. (Prov. 4:5)
Wisdom is the principal thing. (Prov. 4:7)

In bringing up our children, we make more decisions every day—and just as important ones as the president of General Motors.

Being a mother means that we need more insight, understanding, and love than in any other job.

For from the moment we bring a baby home from the hospital, decisions begin that are necessary to the child's welfare and being. We have decisions to make when they are babies, then toddlers and first-graders, during their grammar school, high school, and college years, and even as they reach maturity.

It all takes wisdom. We have discussed wisdom before in this book, but now is the time we need it the most. And God has a plan for us to get help and wisdom.

The Amplified Bible tells it in this way:

"If any of you is deficient in wisdom, let him ask of the giving God [who gives] to every one liberally and ungrudgingly, without reproaching or faultfinding, and it will be given him.

"Only it must be in faith that he asks, with no wavering—no hesitating, no doubting. For the one who wavers (hesitates, doubts) is like the billowing surge out at sea, that is blown hither and thither and tossed by the wind.

"For truly, let not such a person imagine that he will receive anything [he asks for] from the Lord,

"[For being as he is] a man of two minds—hesitating, dubious, irresolute—[he is] unstable and unreliable and uncertain about everything (he thinks, feels, decides)." (James 1:5–8, AMP)

There it is, telling us that wisdom is ours if we don't waver or hesitate, if we are not of two minds, unstable, unreliable, or uncertain. In other words, if our faith is firm and strong.

Who needs wisdom more than a mother, a parent? And it is ours for the asking.

The Mother Who Wouldn't Give Up

Lord, help me! (Matt. 15:25, NIV)

One of the most remarkable stories of the Bible is of a mother seeking help for her child.

She is not given a name in the Bible, but she may be called a Syrophoenician woman. This means she was a heathen woman from the coast of Tyre and Sidon, which was then Syria but today is Lebanon. This was an area of great enmity against the Jewish people.

It is important to know who she was and where she was from, for it gives us some insight into why Jesus acted as he did at first.

Jesus, we are told, had come to her area to get away from all the crowds "but he could not be hid." Evidently he was weary from the demands of the crowds and needed rest.

This woman had heard about Jesus—the miracles and healings—and she had a desperate need. Her child was ill—the Bible says with a demon or evil spirit. Sometimes this means epilepsy, but we do not know for sure. We do know that the child was gravely ill, and the mother knew that she had found the Man who could heal her daughter.

Now the custom of the times made it an affront for a woman of her nationality to speak to a Jew. But she called out to Jesus, "Have mercy upon me, O Lord, thou Son of David; my daughter is grievously vexed with a devil."

But Jesus answered her not a word.

Now whether this was because Jesus was tired and resting or because she was a Gentile who worshiped false gods, we do not know. There is a hint that in the hullabaloo of the moment he had not heard her.

But we know that his disciples heard her continual plea for help because they told Jesus: "Send her away. We are tired of hearing her crying after us."

But now Jesus told her he had been sent to the lost sheep of Israel.

That didn't deter her. There was something greater at stake

124

than nationality boundaries. She had a sick child, and like mothers everywhere, she was going to get help for her child. So she fell down and worshiped him and simply said, "Lord, help me!"

Jesus then told her that it wasn't right to take food from the children and give it to the dogs.

Which isn't really as bad as it sounds. In the terminology of the day this meant that Jesus had his priorities and his teachings were for a certain people.

She agreed. But she also added, "But even the dogs eat of the crumbs which fall from the Master's table."

She wanted just a crumb. That's all it would take for her daughter to be well.

Jesus immediately recognized the love and faith of this mother and said, "O woman, great is thy faith: be it unto thee even as thou wilt."

And the woman's child was healed from that moment.

This story speaks of love and persistence. Don't give up. Keep on till the answer comes.

Operating from a Center of Poise

Ye are wise in Christ. (I Cor. 4:10)

As a Christian mother, operating from a center of poise is one of the best gifts you could give your child—and family.

For when you are centered in Christian poise that means no matter what situation presents itself, you have balance and carry on in equilibrium. You are self-possessed, have composure, assurance, dignity. There is a tranquillity and calm within you that helps you make better decisions and handle situations that you thought could never be handled.

Sounds too good to be true? Not if you have all your Christian resources at your command and use them.

As mothers we are called on to make decisions, give advice and direction, discuss problems, listen, help, and have compassionate care under situations that sometimes are less than ideal. With your inner self centered in Christ and with your resources you can make decisions and bring order to your child's life in a way that can lessen conflict.

When you are working from your center of Christian poise and from your resources you never work from a center of anger or strong emotion—even despair. You have the quiet, calm, and loving voice of authority that the child needs.

Remember, you are not doing this on your own, you *can't* do it on your own. If we have to rely on ourselves, we fall far short. But with your resources you are "wise in Christ" and that helps make the difference.

Ideas for Mothers

With the world so competitive and fast-paced, children are having a more difficult time than ever. There is strong peer pressure that can easily lead into the negative through drugs and other unsavories.

I'll share some things that I have found important in rearing my children. I have two "only" children since they were born ten years apart. They were of different eras, yet the problems they shared are universal.

1. Stay close to your resources and teach your children love of God, family, and fellow human beings. And teach your children resources just for them. There might be a time you will think they forget. But they will remember later.

2. Someone said that the best gift you could give a child is a loving father and mother. Present an undivided front—fair, just, and loving. Parents who allow a child to play one parent against the other are undermining their foundation. And it can cause the child emotional conflicts later on that are difficult to deal with.

3. Respect your child's individuality and uniqueness. The child is not a carbon copy of anyone. Shaping gently is fine, but attempting to mold a child into preconceived ideas courts disaster. Allow each child to be him or her self. And help the children reach their potential with this in mind.

4. Children, even into teen years, want discipline, no matter what they say. They test you and it is easier to give in. But in the long run they respect firm and fair rules. Be consistent. Don't make either threats or promises that you can't keep. Discipline children not to crush spirit but to enhance potential.

5. Allow your children the privilege and joy of earning and fulfilling desires. Teach them that hard work is good and a way to achievement and gain. Help them enjoy victories. Show them

that failure is a part of life, but failing doesn't make them a failure.

6. Keep communication lines open, especially in the teen years. And listen, listen, listen. What is the child saying to you by his or her actions? What is the child crying out for? Teenagers' actions always speak louder than words.

7. Be lavish with sincere praise and understanding. Children thrive on praise.

8. Teach your children to respect others, to have good manners and courteous actions. There might be a time when you think they haven't learned *anything!* But just when you think all hope is lost, you will see them suddenly using your teaching. Don't give up.

How to Pray for Your Child

Pray one for another. (James 5:16)
Pray without ceasing. (I Thess. 5:17)

What would a mother do without prayer? It is the sustaining energy for rearing children.

But always pray from strength—not fear.

I know that sounds easier said than done, but your answers come more quickly if you keep fear away.

Pray for the child every morning. There are some mothers who can give their children over to God one time and then they rest easy. If you are like that—and can do it with complete faith, not just "pretend" faith, but complete wholehearted faith—you are fortunate.

But if you are like most mothers, you remember your children in prayer daily. From babies to the time they leave home. And then some.

To pray from strength you must remember God's promises and fill your mind with them. We have covered most of them in this book, and when you say the promises you are reminding and affirming to yourself and establishing the prayer in your mind. For the deeper your belief, the more answers come.

Use the promises that fit the occasion of the prayer. The following is an idea for a prayer:

Father, since we are all your children by faith, and

heirs according to the promise (Gal. 3:26, 29), and you have promised that you are the God of all people and you tell us: "Is anything too hard for me?" (Jer. 32:27, RSV) and you have promised that we may ask for anything in your name and you will do it (John 14:14):

So I now place —————— in your loving care and in your safety knowing that the Holy Spirit will commune in a way with ——————'s spirit, guiding, correcting, imparting wisdom, teaching and giving love and self-esteem and putting —————— on the path to his (or her) highest potential.

We give thanks for the answer. In the name of Jesus and through his love. Amen.

You might add any resources from any of the chapters of this book as needed.

A Child in the Sky

There are many crisis times in rearing a child. The other day a friend of mine said that her daughter came to her and said she was going to make her first parachute jump!

Of course mothers react. Allie told me that her heart at first did a flip-flop, then she relied on her resources and put the situation in the protecting hands of God. And everything went well.

What if your daughter told you she was going to be the first American woman astronaut in space? That is exactly what happened to Sally Ride's mother, Joyce.

Joyce Ride is an unusual woman. She is strong in her faith and reared her daughters to be individuals to do what they must. And both Joyce's daughters have the pioneering spirit.

So when Sally Ride told her parents she would be the first American woman in space, they took it as part of the natural development of their daughter's potential.

It is interesting to note that Joyce and Dale Ride have two daughters who, in their way, are both "children of the sky." For one, Sally, is the astronaut and the first American woman in space and their other daughter, Karen, is a Presbyterian minister who works with the church to expand the hiring of women pastors!

And, Joyce, herself, like her husband, Dale, is a Presbyterian elder. This is quite an accomplishment for Joyce, also.

Both daughters, Karen and Sally, grew up with understanding parental love that allowed them to develop individually without sexual stereotypes.

And what does Joyce Ride say she and Dale did "right" in rearing their daughters? She says they just allowed each child to develop potential naturally and never told them there were things they couldn't do. They taught their daughters to excel, not to conform.

RESOURCES

As you read these resources about mother and child, it is a good thing to review the resources at the end of Chapter 1 on affirming your identity and also the ones at the end of Chapter 8 on love and Chapter 9 on marriage.

IN HIS LOVING-KINDNESS, GOD

Gives children to the childless wife, so that she becomes a happy mother. Hallelujah! Praise the Lord. (Ps. 113:9, TLB)

AND THEN WE ARE TOLD

May the Lord richly bless both you and your children. (Ps. 115:14, TLB)

FOR

Children are a heritage of the LORD. (Ps. 127:3)

AND WHEN HANNAH DEDICATED HER SON, SAMUEL, TO THE LORD SHE SAID

As surely as you live, my lord, I am the woman who stood here beside you praying to the LORD. I prayed for this child, and the LORD has granted me what I asked of him. So now I give him to the LORD. For his whole life he will be given over to the LORD. (I Sam. 1:26–28, NIV)

THEN IN PROVERBS WE LEARN THIS

Teach a child to choose the right path, and when he is older he will remain upon it. (Prov. 22:6, TLB)

AND

The character of even a child can be known by the way he acts—whether what he does is pure and right. (Prov. 20:11, TLB)

AND WE FIND THIS GIVEN TO US AND OUR CHILDREN

Children, obey your parents; this is the right thing to do

because God has placed them in authority over you.

Honor your father and mother. This is the first of God's Ten Commandments that ends with a promise.

And this is the promise: that if you honor your father and mother, yours will be a long life, full of blessing. (Eph. 6:1–3, TLB)

ALSO

Listen to your father's advice and don't despise an old mother's experience. (Prov. 23:22, TLB)

AND

Hear the instruction of thy father, and forsake not the law of thy mother. (Prov. 1:8)

AND GOD IN HIS LOVE SAYS TO US

As a mother comforts her child, so will I comfort you. (Isa. 66:13, NIV)

AND JESUS SHOWS US HOW LOVE EXTENDS THE FAMILY

"Who is my mother, and who are my brothers?" Pointing to his disciples, he said, "Here are my mother and my brothers. For whoever does the will of my Father in heaven is my brother and sister and mother." (Matt. 12:48–50, NIV)

AND BEFORE THE BABY JESUS WAS BORN, ELIZABETH, MARY'S COUSIN, SAID TO HER

Blessed are you among women, and blessed is the child you will bear! But why am I so favored, that the mother of my Lord should come to me? As soon as the sound of your greeting reached my ears, the baby in my womb leaped for joy.

Blessed is she who has believed that what the Lord has said to her will be accomplished! (Luke 1:42–45, NIV)

AND THIS BEAUTIFUL SONG OF ALL TIME WAS SUNG BY MARY, THE MOTHER OF JESUS, AS SHE AWAITED HIS BIRTH

And Mary said: My soul doth magnify the Lord.

And my spirit hath rejoiced in God my Saviour.

For he hath regarded the low estate of his handmaiden: for, behold, from henceforth all generations shall call me blessed.

For he that is mighty hath done to me great things; and holy is his name.

And his mercy is on them that fear him from generation to generation.

He hath showed strength with his arm; he hath scattered the proud in the imagination of their hearts.

He hath put down the mighty from their seats, and exalted them of low degree.

He hath filled the hungry with good things; and the rich he hath sent empty away.

He hath holpen his servant Israel, in remembrance of his mercy;

And he spake to our fathers, to Abraham, and to his seed for ever. (Luke 1:46–55)

11
WORK, GOALS, AND DREAMS

The Need to Fulfill Potential

Why Dreams Are Healthy

They that seek the LORD shall not want any good thing. (Ps. 34:10)

Dust off your dreams! they are healthy. You are never too old or too young to achieve. To fulfill your potential.

Have you some secret desire, some dream, something that you have always wanted to do? Now is the time to get started. For your dream or desire is God tapping on the door of your heart to announce something good that is waiting for you.

Perhaps you know there is something more out there for you to do, but you don't know what it is. Something that God has in mind for you to accomplish or achieve. It is nagging you in the back of your mind, as when you awake in the morning and a dream has slipped out of your mind. You can see a corner of it, catch a phrase, remember a feeling, but you don't have the whole picture.

Before you are through with this chapter, I will give you ways to find your dream, to find that which you would like to accomplish—pulling it out of your subconscious in a way that is right for you. And also give you the resources to back it up.

What would the world be without dreamers? Those who have put their dreams into action have produced the great inventions, buildings, books, paintings, factories, cities. Everything that is worthwhile and necessary on earth came into being through someone's goals, dreams, or desires.

Some people began with an impossible dream. They were told that it couldn't be done. But they had the audacity to continue, for they found that what a person can believe, a person can achieve.

What Do You Want?

Delight thyself also in the LORD; and he shall give thee the desires of thine heart. (Ps. 37:4)

What do you desire?

A new job? A better position where you are? To work part-time? To paint that picture? To write that book? To sing that new song? (Do *you* have Scripture to back you up!)

Perhaps you are a homemaker who wants to be able to handle the home more efficiently. Or do you want a new car, perhaps even a new home? To begin a business? Part-time work at home?

Do you want to travel? Do you wish to grow more spiritually? To learn more? To help the poor? To feed the hungry? To help the old and lonely?

Nothing is impossible to a person who has a dream and is willing to work to make it come true. Some dreams come true quickly; others can take a lifetime to complete.

Dreams are nudges from God. That is the only way he gets his work done on earth. He puts a dream into a person's heart, and if the individual is willing, he gives him or her the strength and ability to fulfill it.

These Scriptures show you that you will receive all the help necessary:

"[Not in your own strength] for it is God Who is all the while effectually at work in you—energizing and creating in you the power and desire—both to will and to work for His good pleasure and satisfaction and delight.

"Do all things without grumbling and faultfinding and complaining [against God] and questioning and doubting [among yourselves]." (Phil. 2:13–14, AMP)

When God is working something out in our lives, he gives us the ability, power, and strength to carry it forward. All the resources of the Kingdom are ours, if we only believe!

The Secret of the Ages

In the 1920s a man advertised in magazines and newspapers that he had found the secret to success. He said he had studied and worked the laws of success all his life and he had stumbled onto the answer. He could now tell anyone how to become successful and rich. He said this was a universal formula, for every rich person in the world consciously or unconsciously used this formula.

Since the formula had treated him so well, for he was very wealthy, he was willing to share it. He had made his millions and was growing older so it was time to give others the secret. So he was advertising in magazines and newspapers all over the nation so anyone could have the secret.

The secret wasn't free. He was charging for it. For, he said, he had also learned that if something worthwhile is given free, it was human nature not to appreciate it. So anyone could have the secret of the ages for only fifty dollars.

Now fifty dollars was a lot of money in those days. But like the advertiser said, it wasn't much for the secret to success and wealth.

There was a picture in the ad: a small wooden chest that contained the secret. You only had to pay fifty dollars to find out what was in it.

Hundreds of thousands of people sent in their fifty dollars, making the advertiser more millions. Some sent in their money out of curiosity, but the majority really wanted to become successful and wealthy.

When the people received their chest and opened it, they found it was lined in purple velvet. And lying on the plush velvet was a slip of paper with these words:

FIND A NEED AND FILL IT. THE GREATER THE NEED, THE GREATER THE REWARD. GOOD LUCK!

Many were infuriated. Like some people they wanted something for nothing. Instant success. But a few took the formula seriously. They filled a need and became wealthy.

The person who invented the safety pin filled a need, the zipper, the electric light, the telephone, the laundromat, the typewriter. People wanted to travel faster and with more comfort than a horse and buggy, so the car came into being. Then let's skip generations and remember when offices were inundated with paperwork. Stockrooms were in chaos. Then the computer was invented. Among many things it stores information, controls inventory, making it easier to control all facets of a business. Then it was time for computers in smaller sizes that could hold more information which brought microcomputers into being. And on and on.

The world never runs out of needs. For when a need is filled it often creates more needs. And the chain continues.

This book was written out of a need. For years I have wished to be able to give those with whom I counseled, or friends, or neighbors a book that told a Christian woman exactly what resources she had.

It would be a book that told women they were richer than they thought. That gave them hope from a Christian viewpoint and showed them how to use their resources. That told them no matter what the situation, there was an answer. God cares. And he has made provisions for that care.

I envisioned a book that crossed denominational lines, yet stayed with Christian basics. That could help the young woman just emerging but also the older woman, even one in a retirement home or a nursing home. A book that when given as a gift would enhance the potential of both the giver and the receiver.

And so, nurtured in prayer, this book came about.

Look about you for needs. Especially at situations where you have been frustrated about something and said, "Why don't they . . . ?"

You could have found a need.

Fulfilling a Need on a Grand Scale

Write the vision. (Hab. 2:2)

In Chapter 5, "Prayer Refreshment," I told you part of the story of Mary Kay Ash and how her multimillion-dollar company, Mary Kay Cosmetics, Inc., came into being.

How she had decided to write a book incorporating everything she had learned in twenty-five years of direct selling. And how, in writing her book, she realized that she had written the perfect marketing plan to begin a direct sales company.

Mary Kay had "written the vision," the plan, the blueprint. It fueled her imagination. Why not begin her own company?

She looked around for a product that fulfilled a need. Immediately she thought of a skin cream she was using. It worked wonders. A woman was making it, hadn't really perfected it completely, because it still had the consistency of axle grease.

But it worked and would fulfill one of the greatest needs a woman had. To look better and keep her face moisturized so wrinkles would be delayed many years.

So Mary Kay bought the rights to the cream, worked to refine it and bottle it. It took all the money she had.

By this time her husband became involved in the business. He was going to handle the administration part.

One month to the day before they were to open, Mary Kay's husband died of a heart attack at the breakfast table.

Seemingly all her dreams and plans were gone, for she had no money to continue.

After the funeral she and her two sons and daughter held a meeting. They all wanted her to go on with the dream. One of her sons handed her his savings account book with $4,500 in it. He said, "Mom, you can do it!"

With such faith behind her along with her faith in God, how could she fail?

It was tough at first. They began with a little store-front operation. It involved work, work, and more work. But they kept on and kept growing.

Today, nearly twenty years later, Mary Kay heads a multimillion-dollar organization. Nearly 200,000 women work for her as independent contractors and sell her skin-care program through home demonstration parties.

And Mary Kay's slogan is still: "God first, family second, and business third!"

When you keep your life in that order, she says, everything works. If you get your priorities confused or out of order, nothing seems to go right.

Mary Kay fulfills several needs, both for her employees and for her customers. A few are:

1. Every woman has the desire to look better. Prettier. Younger.

2. Her marketing plan gives an average woman, even one with little education, an opportunity—a chance to make as much money as she can. There is no limit on income if you have sales ability and are willing to work.

3. The job fulfills a need for a woman to express herself and a basic need for praise and recognition. Mary Kay says she praises her employees to success. There are incentives every step of the way—diamonds, minks, pink Cadillacs. One of the symbols of the company is a bumblebee. For according to the laws of aerodynamics, a bumblebee is not constructed to fly. But since the bumblebee doesn't know this, it flies anyway. A diamond bumblebee is one of the highest honors of the company.

So dreams are made to be lived.

Needs are there to be fulfilled.

This is an area where everyone has equal opportunity. All you need is a dream or a goal and the desire to fulfill it.

How to Find or Clarify a Dream or Desire

The desire of the righteous shall be granted. (Prov. 10:24)

Perhaps many of you know your dream. It is clear and sharp in your mind. You are fortunate.

There are others who are not so sure, or perhaps torn between more than one dream. And still others who have their dream buried somewhere in their subconscious, and it needs to be pulled out.

For there is an old saying that if you are out in a boat and don't know where you are going, no wind that blows is the right wind. You must have a clear goal.

The following techniques are easy to follow. They will allow you to learn much about yourself, including clarifying your dream, stimulate imagination, and while bringing desires to the fore, they will also help you find talents that you didn't know you had.

All you will need is a notebook divided into four sections and a few minutes of your time daily.

Section 1: Dreams, Desires, and Wishes

In this section write your dreams, desires, and every wish you have. Take your time and write EVERYTHING. It might take you several months to pull them out. There is no hurry. You might find something that catches your "vision" in such a way that it pushes everything else aside. Once you begin, you will find that desires and dreams are stirred up from the most unexpected places. Pray for enlightenment and guidance as you go along.

Section 2: Talents

Write down in this section *every* accomplishment that you ever had that you were proud of. Make it at least fifty to one hundred. Again, there is no hurry. The more you write, the more you will remember. Put a star beside the ones that gave you the feeling inside of "Wow! Did I really do something!"

If you are over twenty-five years of age and you cannot find at least forty accomplishments, review the first chapter of this book and work on your self-image as a child of God.

Section 3: Imagination Plus Emotional Concern

In this section you are allowed to go wild. Let your imagination roam and write down things you would like to do IF THERE WERE NO LIMITS in your life. Pretend you have all the money you need—all human power.

Here you become like the Queen in *Alice in Wonderland* who believed in as many as six impossible things before breakfast. You're going to do better. You will probably have a hundred or more by the time you finish. Think big. Don't dream small dreams.

Play with this. Have fun. Before long you will see a pattern emerging in your imagination patterns. And your concerns and dislikes in life. And you will find out something else about yourself. Your life is dyed the color of your imagination. You can get quite emotional with these dreams as you go along. Take your time and have at least twenty-five to fifty.

Section 4: The Vision

When you have worked with the first three sections until you can't get another drop of information, then you can begin to cull. But be sure you have passed a point in your mind on all three sections where you have worked until you have heard a little "click" in your mind. That is when you break through to depths of the mind you seldom use.

From Section 1 put down the desires or dreams, or perhaps you will have only one. Have you already found it?

From Section 2 write the accomplishments that stand out in your life. Do you see a pattern? It could help tell you where your talents lie. Or where you need to make up a deficiency.

From Section 3 write down the wildest dreams that affect you emotionally—things that you want to get on your soapbox about. Changes that you feel deeply about.

Now that you have written all this down, patterns should emerge. If you need help with the final desire, the following Scripture is a good one to affirm as a promise:

"Commit thy works unto the LORD and thy thoughts shall be established" (Prov. 16:3).

Put Your Dream Into Action

Once you have clarified your dream, then it is time to put it into action. With much prayer for guidance and wisdom.

These women put their dreams into action. They followed their dream and it brought fulfillment into their lives.

1. Marcie was always frustrated when she couldn't buy a good organic whole wheat bread. So she baked her own. Soon friends and neighbors were lining up to buy her bread, and she had a thriving business out of her home. Now the business has grown so that she is moving into a shop and is distributing her wheat, rye, and corn bread on a citywide basis. The way orders are coming in, next year she could be selling statewide.

2. Jessica's dream is to paint. She is a frustrated artist and in the past hadn't even done any sketching. But it was not too late to begin. She put herself in the hands of an arts-and-crafts store and they outfitted her with sketchbook, charcoal, paints, canvas, and easel.

She is as happy as can be, taking lessons now and learning her craft. Who knows what it will lead to? The enjoyment of working at her dream is all she is looking for at this time.

Jessica is eighty.

3. Josie's dream was to travel. And for that she needed money. She didn't want to work full time, because she wanted to be home with her teenagers.

She was told that her frustrations could tell her something about needs. And her pet peeve was that she could never find a good yard person in the summer when her boys were not available. And if she did find one the work often was sloppy.

So Josie enlisted her two teenage boys, who were now old enough to help, and their friend and went into a summer lawn-mowing business.

Their first equipment was the family's mower and edger, and her son's old battered pickup provided the transportation. The boys provided the labor and Josie attended to the business details and advertising and sweeping up and being general helper.

She used quick-copy printing for handbills they distributed in the neighborhood, advertised in the shopping news and on free bulletin boards, and put a cheap magnetic sign on the truck.

This is Josie's third year and she is booked up for the summer. She works three months and made enough even the first year to pay the boys good wages and have enough left over for Josie and her husband to take a trip to Bermuda. Last year it was Europe and this year it will be Israel with a side trip to Egypt.

4. Deanna has a little girl two years old named Lia. Deanna's dream was for Lia to have special school and friends to play with. They live in a small town and there is nothing like this available.

So Deanna began a play school in her home for Lia and four other children. Deanna is innovative and is a loving and caring young mother. Already there is a waiting list for her school.

Look about you and you will see many stories of people fulfilling their dreams.

Faith without works is dead. Dreams without action are worthless. Once you make a decision to put your dream into action it is no longer idle fancy. It becomes a goal with a pathway leading toward it. Realize that exercising your talent is part of God's plan for you.

It is time to begin.

Persistence Is the Key

Cast your cares on the LORD,
and he will sustain you;
he will never let the righteous fall. (Ps. 55:22, NIV)

When you find the path to your goal, be determined to press on. Accept the promises of your rich Christian heritage. Nothing is too good for a child of the Kingdom. Don't settle for second best.

And your success depends on how you keep the negatives out. It takes persistence. If we let our faith down, become easily discouraged or weary, we can lose the battle. Enlist your will. Set it in the right direction through prayer.

Many people just begin to grasp the meaning of living in the Kingdom. They begin with high hopes to solve problems, improve conditions in their life, or further a goal.

Then when the desires don't immediately come to pass, they go back to the old ways. They didn't realize the value of persistence as taught in the Bible. Remember the story that Jesus told of the man knocking (Luke 11:5–10)? And then his great promises of "ask, seek, and knock"? The verbs are in a tense that means "keep on asking, keep on seeking, and keep on knocking."

"Ask and keep on asking, and it shall be given you; seek and keep on seeking, and you shall find; knock and keep on knocking, and the door shall be opened to you." (Luke 11:9, AMP)

Don't give up. Keep on. Your answer will come.

The following quotation by Calvin Coolidge long has been a favorite of mine:

> Nothing in the world can take the place of persistence. Talent will not: nothing is more common than unsuccessful people with talent. Genius will not: unrewarded genius is almost a proverb. Education alone will not: the world is full of educated derelicts. Persistence and determination alone are omnipotent.

So you take a woman who knows her Christian resources and who adds persistence and determination and you have an unbeatable combination leading to success.

RESOURCES

These resources will help you not only in finding success but also in every other area of your life. You can combine them with resources from any other chapter in this book, or you can use them alone. For they bring out the best in us, showing that when we live in the Kingdom all that is good will be ours.

DESIRES, DREAMS, AND GOALS ARE IMPORTANT, FOR WE ARE TOLD

Delight thyself also in the LORD; and he shall give thee the desires of thine heart.

Commit thy way unto the LORD; trust also in him; and he shall bring it to pass. (Ps. 37:4–5)

FOR

There is a time for every purpose and for every work. (Eccl. 3:17)

SO

Commit your work to the Lord, then it will succeed. (Prov. 16:3, TLB)

SO WE SAY

I love the LORD, because he hath heard my voice and my supplications.

Because he hath inclined his ear unto me, therefore will I call upon him as long as I live. (Ps. 116:1–2)

AND WE KNOW TO

Trust in the LORD with all thine heart; and lean not unto thine own understanding.

In all thy ways acknowledge him, and he shall direct thy paths. (Prov. 3:5–6)

I ALSO KNOW

My help cometh from the LORD, which made heaven and earth. (Ps. 121:2)

For the word of the LORD is right; and all his works are done in truth. (Ps. 33:4)

AND

The desire of the righteous shall be granted. (Prov. 10:24)

Thou hast given him his heart's desire, and hast not withholden the request of his lips. (Ps. 21:2)

FOR
> You open your hand and satisfy the desires of every living thing. (Ps. 145:16, NIV)

> If we ask any thing according to his will, he heareth us. (I John 5:14)

SO HE TELLS US
> What things soever ye desire, when ye pray, believe that ye receive them, and ye shall have them. (Mark 11:24)

FOR
> Every good and perfect gift is from above, coming down from the Father of the heavenly lights, who does not change like shifting shadows. (James 1:17, NIV)

AND WE KNOW
> All things work together for good to them that love God. (Rom. 8:28)

SO
> If God be for us, who can be against us? (Rom. 8:31)

> Cast your cares on the LORD, and he will sustain you; he will never let the righteous fall. (Ps. 55:22, NIV)

> For those who seek the LORD lack no good thing. (Ps. 34:10, NIV)

FOR HE TELLS US
> I will go before thee, and make the crooked places straight. (Isa. 45:2)

> In quietness and in confidence shall be your strength. (Isa. 30:15)

SO I KNOW
> He is my rock and my fortress. (Ps. 71:3)

AND
> He set my feet upon a rock, and established my goings. (Ps. 40:2)

AND I
> Stand fast in the faith. (I Cor. 16:13)

AND
> I can do all things through Christ which strengtheneth me. (Phil. 4:13)

AND I HEED THE ADMONITION
> Where there is no vision, the people perish. (Prov. 29:18)

SO WHEN WE LIVE UP TO OUR POTENTIAL WE ARE
TOLD

Well done, thou good and faithful servant:

thou hast been faithful over a few things, I will make thee ruler
over many things: enter thou into the joy of thy lord. (Matt.
25:21)

12
A SAFE HAVEN
The Need for Security

A Sure Thing

We all want security—a safe haven. Something we can depend on.

How about being able to sail your yacht into a lovely lagoon on a tropical island? A safe harbor where you will be taken care of for the rest of your life, financially, emotionally, and intellectually. You live in a special cocoon that is built about you and you are safe, protected, and loved.

Now that we have heard the fairy tale, let's deal with reality. For that isn't what happens to most of us on earth. Hurricanes come and sink boats. Stocks and bonds drop. Buildings crumble. Relationships end. Conditions change.

But, as Christian women, we know our security lies in things of the Spirit. Our own indwelling strength has the imprint of God upon our life. When we are able to handle anything that comes our way.

That is true security.

Treasures on Earth

Lay not up for yourselves treasures upon earth. (Matt. 6:19)

Roberta is a friend of mine. She has enough money to last her ten lifetimes, yet she lives in the terror of insecurity. She is afraid that her money will be taken away from her or she won't have enough. She could travel, enjoy herself, do any of a dozen

145

interesting things, including helping those about her. Yet she lives in fear. She has put all her faith in her money, and what if it fails her?

Roberta is intelligent enough to know that money can disappear, buildings tumble, and whole cities can be destroyed by earthquake and fire. In fact that is Roberta's fear. She lives in California, where recently there was an earthquake not one hundred miles from her.

She constantly frets. What if the bank collasped? Interest rates are too high. Inflation and taxes are eating up her assets. Roberta is a good example of "where your treasure is, there will your heart be also" (Matt. 6:21).

No matter how much money Roberta has, it will never be enough—in her present state of mind. So far no one has been able to change her thinking pattern.

Now there is nothing wrong with having money. It is a valid medium of exchange in our world and we need it to survive. Money, used rightly, can bring freedom and help. It is the wrong use, or "the love of money," that presents the problem. Misunderstanding the purpose of money can become a prison, as it is for Roberta. With all her assets, Roberta has not found peace. She has more than enough money, but no security. Roberta is a most miserable person.

Treasures in Heaven—Where True Security Is

Lay up for yourselves treasures in heaven, where neither moth nor rust doth corrupt, and where thieves do not break through nor steal. (Matt. 6:20)

Where does true security lie? That is easily answered if you are a Christian woman. For no matter what type of security you are seeking—for finances, for your body or emotions—security lies in the spiritual assets you build into your mind.

Our security lies in the fact that we recognize that we are children of God and have all the attributes of the Kingdom. We have within us all the strength that is necessary to meet any challenge that life presents.

Our security lies in using our talents—our capabilities—in the knowledge that we are in control through Christ. That no matter what life presents to us, we have our inner resources and we can go on. We can rebuild if we must.

The story of Donnie tells us this. Donnie was an eleven-year-old who was as brown as a butternut with freckles that danced all over his nose when he smiled. We met him on the beach at Galveston Island, where we had rented a house one summer.

Every morning when we arrived at the beach, we found Donnie already busy building his sand castles. When we came back after lunch and a siesta, Donnie would still be there, intently working. He wore a white T-shirt over his suit, which he kept wet by running for a plunge in the surf every few minutes. Then Donnie would come back and continue building his castle. He was serious. You could see the concentration on his face as he worked.

Every day Donnie built a bigger and better sand castle. This particular one had towers and turrets which he smoothed out carefully with his red sand shovel. He even dug a moat around the castle to make it look more authentic.

I walked over to Donnie, complimenting him on his work. "It's a beautiful castle—fine job, Donnie."

He shyly acknowledged me with a nod.

I could see that the tide was coming in. In a few hours Donnie's sand castle would be gone.

"Donnie," I asked, "how can you stand to see all your hard work already washed away?"

"Oh, it's O.K." he said, his eyes lighting up. "I've always got my shovel." He held up his sand shovel. "And there's plenty of sand."

Donnie spoke a great truth: his security wasn't in the sand castle he built, and it really wasn't in the red shovel he had, for that shovel without someone to use it was just a tool. Donnie's security was in himself—the knowledge that he was capable of building more castles, more and bigger ones out of the plenty of sand that was there.

So the Christian woman who believes in her resources and her ability to use them has her shovel and plenty of sand.

As Christian women we have learned that from the invisible comes the visible. There are enough ideas in the universe—for idea begats idea—to keep us all busy. And there are enough needs to be filled to give us all a job. And our supply and our

147

security come from our willingness to work, from knowing that we have what it takes, no matter what experiences we meet along the way.

Affirming Our Security

Hold thou me up, and I shall be safe. (Ps. 119:117)

I have found the following points helpful in affirming and understanding true security, whether it is financial, bodily, or emotional.

1. Your security is affirmed by the fact that you are a child of the King. You are an inheritor of the Kingdom. As a Christian you have within you everything you need to cope with anything life has to offer. The greater your sense of self-worth as a child of God, the greater your security. The more receptive we are to God's Spirit within us, the taller we stand knowing we have resources to meet any demand put upon us.

2. Your security lies in understanding that every adversity holds within it a possibility for good. So adversity should never make a Christian woman feel inadequate.

The adversary has thrown down the gauntlet, but you are calm and confident, for you have all the resources you need to be an overcomer. And you will find that your confidence and inner strength multiply as you use them. Faith muscles develop firm and strong. Nothing from the negative can best you.

So look for the seed in every circumstance that "means it for good." It is there.

3. Your security is in the fact that as a Christian you are never alone. Sometimes the enemy tries to whisper to you that you are alone and deserted by everyone. And you often feel that it might be true—our family is busy, our friends have gone their way.

But in reality you are never alone. God is always with us. His loving care and support is there to blend with us, help us and give us strength and comfort.

The moment we turn within and seek his presence, we can feel a calmness, a serenity—a security found in no other way. So allow him to comfort you, bring sustenance to you. There is a key to the word "allow," for God does not violate your privacy. He is standing at the door knocking, but you must open that door and invite him in.

4. True security with God as your partner means that you are never afraid to step out, to begin new projects. You now can say "Yes!" to life. Your security is in yourself and your resources to try new ways, make new pathways, put your dreams into action.

Life becomes more of an adventure than ever because you are not depending on others as you might have had to in the past. You are depending on *you* and the strength that God gives you. Your security lies in yourself and in your resources to do what you wish. And you do not put your security in one situation, one circumstance, job, or person—but in your Source and you.

5. Your security lies in the fact that you are not afraid of tomorrow, what it might bring, for your hand is in God's hand and all is well.

You eagerly look forward to tomorrow and your good that it will bring. You are not unsure of the way. You are confident and unafraid, for God knows the way. The psalmist spoke of this feeling of being protected and guided when he said God was a "lamp to his feet and a light to his path" (Ps. 119:105, RSV).

So affirm God's loving protection and guidance. We can meet all things with courage, for God is with us.

Lift your eyes up from where your help comes. He is eternally vigilant, neither slumbering nor sleeping. He will keep you safe, for "the LORD is thy keeper" (Ps. 121:5).

This makes you not afraid of the future because you accept change as part of life and it is always welcome. When you look at change through the eyes of faith it always brings that which is more desirable to you.

6. Finally, your security lies in the fact that wherever you are, God is.

We are eternally enfolded in God's presence. We are directed, guided, and protected whether traveling, staying at home, working, playing—whatever we do God is with us. We are safe and secure.

There is a beautiful prayer of protection written by James Dillet Freeman. He is the poet who wrote the inspiring poem that the astronauts carried to the moon at the first landing.

It goes like this:

> The light of God surrounds me;
> The love of God enfolds me;

The power of God protects me;
The presence of God watches over me.
Wherever I am, God is!

Probably Henry van Dyke summed it all up when he was asked to define security. He said:

Faith to believe,
work to enjoy, and
someone to love.

RESOURCES

True security in God means to let go of past, present, and future—and trust. The following promises will show you the way. After you read and meditate on them it is good to finish with the resources in Chapter 6 on praise and thanksgiving. Always give thanks for what you wish to receive, for with faith you see it already accomplished.

WE ARE TOLD

Trust in him at all times, O people; pour out your hearts to him, for God is our refuge. (Ps. 62:8, NIV)

YES, WE KNOW

The eternal God is your refuge, and underneath are the everlasting arms. (Deut. 33:27, NIV)

SO WE AFFIRM

The LORD is my strength and song, and he is become my salvation. (Ex. 15:2)

He giveth power to the faint; and to them that have no might he increaseth strength. (Isa. 40:29)

SO

I will lift up mine eyes unto the hills, from whence cometh my help. (Ps. 121:1)

AND WE RELAX BECAUSE

Whoso putteth his trust in the LORD shall be safe. (Prov. 29:25)

FOR

Then shalt thou walk in thy way safely, and thy foot shall not stumble. (Prov. 3:23)

For in the day of trouble, he will keep me safe in his dwelling;

he will hide me in the shelter of his tabernacle and set me high upon a rock. (Ps. 27:5, NIV)

AND HE PROMISES

All who listen to me shall live in peace and safety, unafraid. (Prov. 1:33, TLB)

Never will I leave you; never will I forsake you. (Heb. 13:5, NIV)

FOR HE PROMISES

My presence will go with you. (Ex. 33:14, RSV)

For I the LORD thy God will hold thy right hand, saying unto thee, Fear not; I will help thee. (Isa. 41:13)

AND

I will make darkness light before them, and crooked things straight. These things will I do unto them, and not forsake them. (Isa. 42:16)

SO

Cast all your anxiety on him because he cares for you. (I Peter 5:7)

For he will command his angels concerning you to guard you in all your ways. (Ps. 91:11, NIV)

SO REMEMBER TO

Be strong in the Lord, and in the power of his might.
Put on the whole armor of God. (Eph. 6:10–11)

FOR WE KNOW TO

Find rest, O my soul, in God alone; my hope comes from him.
He alone is my rock and my salvation; he is my fortress, I will not be shaken.
My salvation and my honor depend on God; he is my mighty rock, my refuge.
Trust in him at all times, O people; pour out your hearts to him, for God is our refuge. (Ps. 62:5–8, NIV)

SO THIS MEANS

The beloved of the LORD shall dwell in safety by him. (Deut. 33:12)

FOR

He that dwelleth in the secret place of the Most High shall abide under the shadow of the Almighty. I will say of the LORD, He is my refuge and my fortress; my God; in him will I trust. (Ps. 91:1–2)

13
LIVING WITH COURAGE
The Need to Banish Fear

Living in the Right Kingdom

Fear hath torment. He that feareth is not made perfect in love.
There is no fear in love; but perfect love casteth out fear. (I
John 4:18)

Fear, irrational fear, is one of the most insidious of the negatives; in fact, fear is the foundational negative. It is part of the
gang from the adversary that I call "the unholy three"—fear,
worry, and anxiety.

Now I am not talking about natural fear, which is given to warn
us of danger. No, I am talking about the irrational fears that tear
us apart—for nothing. They make us miserable and attempt to
rule our life. Fear is one of the adversary's favorite tricks—to ruin
our life, to take the shine off our joy.

This chapter was put in this place in my book for a reason—so
you would know enough of our Christian resources before you
would handle fear. For if you are caught in a fear trap, you will
need them all.

As you deal with fear, you will realize that fear tricks us. It has
no power over us, except what we give it. For as fear attempts to
sap our energies, faith restores them. Fear subtracts from life, but
faith and courage and all that is good from God restore and add
to life. For God is our courage, our security, strength, guide, and
protection.

Fear knocked at our door.
Faith answered.
There was no one there.

Recognizing the True Kingdom

For as a man thinketh in his heart, so is he. (Prov. 23:7)

There is no truth in him [the adversary], . . . for he is a liar and the father of lies. (John 8:44, RSV)

I wish I had the space to approach this subject more delicately, pack it in feathers, but you are a Christian woman with a knowledge of your resources, so perhaps it is good I don't.

For the truth is—if you continue to live in fear day after day, you are living in the kingdom of the adversary. Living the way of the kingdom of fear is a sin—you are "missing the mark." For when you have irrational fears, worries, or anxiety, you are putting your faith in evil. You believe more in the negative than in the Sonshine. You believe more in the adversary than in God. You are believing more in the father of lies than in our Father in heaven.

So, again, as a believer, you are put into a position where you must choose: "Choose you this day whom ye will serve" (Josh. 24:15).

In a fear situation, you don't wait for circumstances to change. You follow your resources and *change circumstances.* You begin to trust God completely. You turn over every concern to God. You begin to pray and use praise—the universal antidote. You affirm your identity as a child of God and what it means and the authority it has given you. You stir up your faith, use strong Scripture power, and stand firm.

For when a Christian woman is properly related to God, she has within her all the ingredients to live richly and fully and in joy, peace, and harmony. You choose.

Oh, the vultures of fear might fly over you, even attempt to rest momentarily. But you don't have to allow them to build a nest in your hair. Fear will tug at you, but rout it out—now!

Fear always puts a Christian to the test. Remember Job? He said, "For the thing which I greatly feared is come upon me, and

153

that which I was afraid of is come unto me" (Job 3:25). Fear can draw the negative. So do we believe, or don't we? Distorted thinking will undermine you. So put your mind on God and stand firm.

For you as a Christian woman are a conqueror, an overcomer. You win because you set your will and mind toward faith. And you recognize the true Kingdom of God and don't allow yourself to be tricked by the enemy.

In Darkness a Lie Believed Becomes a Truth to Us

For ye were sometime in darkness, but now are ye light in the Lord: walk as children of light. (Eph. 5:8)

Fear has a trick that at one time or another deceives us all. What we fear and believe in—whether true or not—rules us and becomes a truth to us.

Remember, it doesn't have to be true—it can be a lie—yet if we believe, we live it as a truth.

One evening I was taking a walk after dark and saw what I thought was a snake coiled by the side of the walkway. I didn't know it was only a piece of rope. I thought it was a snake. Did I react to what really was there or to what I *believed* was there? You know the answer to that one.

I froze, seeing the "snake," and adrenaline began pumping into my body. My whole system revved up in a split second, preparing me for "flight or fight." And flight it was, for I got away from there pronto!

Not only did I believe I saw a snake, but I allowed my imagination to add to my fears. I was "sure" I had seen a copperhead that had crawled up from the creek.

It wasn't until the next day as I gingerly walked the same path, in the light, that I found the same "snake" coiled by the path.

All that fear for nothing. All that churning of the system for nothing.

How often do we run from (or stay and fight) false fears. How often are we ruled by our "mistaken certainties" that do adverse things to body, mind, and spirit.

So examine your fear beliefs. How many are real and how

many are false? Expose the counterfeit to the Light. It will disappear.

How Fear Attempts to Rule Us

For God hath not given us the spirit of fear; but of power, and of love, and of a sound mind. (II Tim. 1:7)

There are many fears in the trap of the unholy three: fear, worry, and anxiety. We find everything from fear of failure, fear of what the neighbors might think, fear of rejection, fear of being found inadequate to fear of change. Let's look these fears right in the eye and recognize our enemy.

1. *Fear divides the mind.*
"Every kingdom divided against itself will be ruined, and every city or household divided against itself will not stand." (Matt. 12:25, NIV)
A divided mind cannot accomplish anything. It loses its strength and becomes weak. The enemy wins the battle when we allow him to come in and divide our mind. Be alert and close the gap with your resources.

2. *Fear makes the emotions unstable and brings doubt.*
"He who doubts is like a wave of the sea, blown and tossed by the wind. . . . He is a double-minded man, unstable in all he does." (James 1:6, 8, NIV)
When fear rules, your life becomes unstable and irrational, and you are unable to stand firm in the face of adversity. It also breaks your line to your resources, for now your dominant factor is from the negative. When your connection to your Source is cut and your mind becomes unstable, we are told: "That man should not think he will receive anything from the Lord" (James 1:7, NIV).
So go in and "take possession of the land" (Josh. 1:11, RSV). Take back what you have given over to the enemy. Stand firm and don't allow the enemy to stay any longer.

3. *Fear takes our persistence away.*
"Blessed is the man who perseveres." (James 1:12, NIV)
Persistence, determination, and being able to stand firm are all

attributes a Christian woman needs to be an overcomer. The unholy three attempt to rob you of your ability to stand strong. So shore up the sides, lock the gate with your resources.

4. *Fear paralyzes the will.*

"For if the willingness is there, the gift is acceptable." (II Cor. 8:12, NIV)

With fear in your life, you have abdicated your will. You have given control into the enemy's hands. You are no longer ruler of your own household. Fear has made your will a stooge of the enemy.

Refuse to think fear thoughts. Put your will into God's domain by a deliberate act of will.

5. *Fear robs you of your joy.*

"The joy of the LORD is your strength." (Neh. 8:10)

Fear can rob you of daily joy. It can make your life so miserable that you live in constant gloom. As a Christian, practice your resources and you will have a deep and abiding joy regardless of circumstances. Fear attempts to break that line.

6. *Fear can rob us of our health.*

"Know ye not that your body is the temple of the Holy Ghost which is in you, which ye have of God, and ye are not your own?" (I Cor. 6:19)

Fear can bring a breakdown of our body. It can upset the balance of the physical body, which can result in illness. Irrational fear, worry, and anxiety are directly from the pit of the enemy. Get them out of your life.

How to Fight Fear

Be not overcome of evil, but overcome evil with good. (Rom. 12:21)

The other evening Edward and I were in the kitchen talking. We had the back door open and suddenly we heard a commotion in the alley at the garbage cans.

We looked at each other, immediately knowing what it was—

raccoons! Often they come up from the creek and decide to forage in the alley.

It was a cloudy night and pitch-black out there. Did Edward go out and fight the darkness, box with the night, or make a battle with the dark?

Of course not, but that is what many of us do with the negative, the fears, worries, and concerns.

No, Edward ran for his flashlight and turned on the patio light and went back into the alley. Shining his light on the raccoons and with a couple of "shoo's," they fled.

Never fight fear. That is one of the tricks of the adversary, trying to get you engaged in combat. Fighting a negative only intensifies it. It gets energy from our fighting.

Replace the unholy three with prayer and praise. Turn on the Sonlight. That is the way to overcome darkness.

How to Overcome Fear and Its Cohorts

I will trust, and not be afraid; for the LORD GOD is my strength and my song. (Isa. 12:2, RSV)

Fear and its cohorts can cripple your life. The following are some ways I have found to overcome:

1. Take charge of your thinking. Your mind can only think of one thing at a time. You *choose*. Use any of the resources in this book that give you comfort and help.

2. Analyze your fears. Then do what you can about them. Put as much energy in working and trusting as you did in being fearful. Fill your mind with praise and thanksgiving.

3. Check your reactions. Have you gotten into the habit of reacting to everything with a fear thought? Learn to react from a Christ center of poise.

4. Build courage and cheerfulness into your spirit by acting the part until it becomes natural. There is a saying that if you "assume a virture for ten days, it becomes yours." Since most of our fears are a habit, build the opposite, courage, into your life.

5. Trust. Are you really, *really* trusting? There isn't a better time to find out how strong your Christian mettle is. Do you believe, or don't you?

Did you know that your ability to trust comes from God? You

157

instigate it but he multiplies it. Trust dissolves fear. It disappears. Trust can banish fear with a song, a prayer, a Scripture—any resource. Once you are on a "trusting level" fear cannot touch you. You will feel free, light, and joyful.

Two Women of Courage

Be of good cheer; I have overcome the world. (John 16:33)

When I think of Christian women of courage, there are many. But the two I have chosen to write about are special women of faith. In fact, without understanding their Christian faith, you can't understand them. They have both gone through adversity and sorrow that would have crushed the average person. Yet, it has made their faith and belief that much stronger.

My women of courage are Rose Kennedy and Dale Evans.

Rose Kennedy has had eight children: four were killed in adulthood and one is retarded. We all know that sons John F. and Robert were assassinated, one when President of the United States and the other when a U.S. Senator. The oldest son, Joseph, Jr., was killed in World War II while flying a special mission. Four years later beautiful Kathleen was killed in a plane crash in the Swiss Alps. Rosemary is retarded and has been institutionalized most of her life.

Dale Evans lost little Robin, the "angel unaware" child of the book of the same name, when she was still a toddler. Sandy, the son who was in the Army, died in a tragic accident in Europe. And daughter Debbie, in the sixth grade, was killed in a church bus accident while on an outing.

When we think of what these women have gone through, we think how easy it would be for them to turn bitter. To live in constant fear of Where will the sword drop next? How easy it would be to doubt God and give in to fear. But that isn't what has happened. They both feel they have emerged from tragedy stronger than ever. Their faith is vibrant and alive.

Of course there are many questions unanswered. But they trust. They are victors—overcomers. They are what we are told to be—"strong in the Lord." Dale Evans says: "Nothing the adversary can do to me shakes my faith. It is firmly rooted in Jesus Christ."

And Rose Kennedy. She says she believes that God wants us to be happy, even in the midst of seemingly unbearable challenges. She says, "Birds sing after a storm, why shouldn't we?"

Peace Comes from God

Thou wilt keep him in perfect peace, whose mind is stayed on thee: because he trusteth in thee. Trust ye in the LORD for ever: for in the LORD JEHOVAH is everlasting strength. (Isa. 26:3–4)

Peace I leave with you, my peace I give unto you. . . . Let not your heart be troubled, neither let it be afraid. (John 14:27)

The first step in any healing, whether fear, anxiety, worry, or even a bodily healing, is to do as the prodigal son said he would do: "I will arise and go to my father" (Luke 15:18).

God is always with us. But we must "arise and go to the Father"—cultivate his presence. We have to make the decision continually, for part of our mind will tug on us to go another way.

When we are caught in a fear trap we must use our free will. We have a right to choose the good, to go the way of the Father. We do not have to listen to the clamoring of fear, of worry, even of the opinions of others.

We can choose and we must choose. We can deny that anything other than God and his good have a place in our life. We can deny what we do not want in our life. Free will gives us the ability to reject that which we do not want. And accept that which we do. This accepting and rejecting is something we don't use often enough. It is a wonderful gift from God. Use it.

And when we do use it, peace comes into our life. Peace is the complete acceptance of God's presence within us, shining with serenity, knowing that regardless of outer conditions all is well.

My Special Phrase

I would like to share with you a special phrase that has added to my faith through the years. Especially in those moments every woman has when a name comes to mind of someone dear and a momentary flick of fear comes with it. Or I often end prayer or

Bible Scripture reading with this phrase. I put the situation or the person:

lovingly in the hands of the Father and all is well.

If you are in a "fear pattern," you can use this phrase a hundred times a day. It can bring faith and comfort in any situation.

RESOURCES

The following resources are on fear, but if you need more, use some from every chapter in this book. Fear needs much ammunition against it. Often we are so programmed that we must work by blind faith alone. That is O.K. until you can get your Christian equilibrium back. Everyone has had those times. Just don't give up. And one day the Sonlight breaks through.

OFTEN

We were troubled on every side; without were fightings, within were fears. (II Cor. 7:5)

BUT

What time I am afraid, I will trust in thee. (Ps. 56:3)

SO

I will lift up mine eyes unto the hills, from whence cometh my help. (Ps. 121:1)

FOR THE LORD TELLS US

But whoso hearkeneth unto me shall dwell safely, and shall be quiet from fear of evil. (Prov. 1:33)

For I the LORD thy God will hold thy right hand, saying unto thee, Fear not; I will help thee. (Isa. 41:13)

AND HE PROMISES US

No weapon that is formed against us shall prosper. . . .

This is the heritage of the servants of the LORD. (Isa. 54:17)

AND WE CAN SAY

I sought the LORD, and he heard me, and delivered me from all my fears. (Ps. 34:4)

FOR WE KNOW

The LORD will keep you from all harm—he will watch over your life; the LORD will watch over your coming and going both now and forevermore. (Ps. 121:7–8, NIV)

The LORD upholds all those who fall and lifts up all who are bowed down. (Ps. 145:14, NIV)

FOR
Great peace have they who love your law, and nothing can make them stumble. (Ps. 119:165, NIV)

SO
Wait on the LORD; be of good courage, and he shall strengthen thine heart: wait, I say, on the LORD. (Ps. 27:14)

AND WE KNOW
The angel of the LORD encampeth round about them that fear him, and delivereth them. (Ps. 34:7)

SO DON'T BE AFRAID BUT
Cast thy burden upon the LORD, and he shall sustain thee. (Ps. 55:22)

FOR WE ARE TOLD
Thou wilt keep him in perfect peace, whose mind is stayed on thee. (Isa. 26:3)

And the peace of God, which passeth all understanding, shall keep your hearts and minds through Christ Jesus. (Phil. 4:7)

SO THE THING TO DO IS TO
Acquaint now thyself with him, and be at peace: thereby good shall come unto thee. (Job 22:21)

Peace I leave with you, my peace I give unto you. (John 14:27)

SO
Cast all your care upon him; for he careth for you. (I Peter 5:7)

SO OUR FEARS ARE PUT TO REST, FOR
There is no fear in love; but perfect love casteth out fear: because fear hath torment. He that feareth is not made perfect in love. (I John 4:18)

SO WE KNOW
The LORD is my light and my salvation; whom shall I fear? The LORD is the strength of my life; of whom shall I be afraid? . . . Though a host should encamp against me, my heart shall not fear. (Ps. 27:1, 3)

SO WE ARE TOLD
Don't be anxious about tomorrow. God will take care of your tomorrow too. Live one day at a time. (Matt. 6:34, TLB)

14
LETTING GOD AND LIVING FREE
The Need to Forgive

Freedom and Forgiveness

Forgive, and you will be forgiven. (Luke 6:37, RSV)
And the truth shall make you free. (John 8:32)
Where the Spirit of the Lord is, there is liberty. (II Cor. 3:17)

The core of Christianity is pure freedom. And it comes from the forgiveness principle that says: As you have been forgiven; you forgive others (Matt. 6:14–15).

In Christianity you are forgiven and you let the past go—every day is a new beginning and you are free! First you acknowledge the forgiveness given to you by God through his son, Jesus, then you pass that same forgiveness on to all those about you by forgiving them.

How many times does this principle work? There is no end to the number of times you forgive and are forgiven. Jesus used the number seventy times seven—a number meaning infinity. So how can we hold anyone in the bondage of unforgiveness and be a follower of his?

Christianity is freedom for everyone through forgiveness. We forgive—and a burden lifts. Something is let go. For forgiveness brings an inner peace. It is releasing the past and living fully, joyfully, thankfully in the present.

Forgiveness is never indifference. Forgiveness comes from a caring and understanding heart, and complete trust in God.

We are told to love our enemies and pray for those who curse us. That is as much for our sake as for those for whom we pray.

For unforgiveness and its cohorts—resentment, anger, revenge, criticism, and condemnation—can corrode and kill the vessel they live in.

Forgiveness is given by us through an act of will. You must *decide* to forgive. It is up to you. And you alone have the power to forgive those whom you are holding in bondage.

Once you look at the world through the eyes of forgiveness, your life changes. For then you are no longer reinforcing guilt, anger, judgment, condemnation, criticism, and resentment. You are looking at the world through the eyes of love.

So without our forgiving others there is no true Christian happiness. You will find that you cannot live the complete Christian abundant life without forgiveness.

Forgiveness is your key to freedom.

The Value of Forgiveness

Create in me a clean heart, O God; and renew a right spirit within me. (Ps. 51:10)

When David cried the above words, asking God for forgiveness, he was setting into motion a powerful principle. For the forgiveness of God is the most powerful therapeutic idea in the world.

Unforgiveness can bring guilt and just about every ill known to humankind. It can make our life miserable and take away our joy and even ruin our potential and talents.

But confession and acceptance of forgiveness can make our life whole again. It is a cleansing, refreshing bath in love from which we emerge radiant, full of energy, and able to live up to our highest good.

Then we take a moment in the joy of forgiveness to reflect on what our forgiveness means. We are forgiven and now we forgive others. We realize what we have to forgive is but a small part of how Jesus forgave.

For who can even comprehend the love and forgiveness of Jesus? In his hour of deepest agony, beaten and tortured, yet his compassion was such that he could look with eyes of love upon his slayers. For in forgiving tenderness he said: "Father, forgive them; for they know not what they do" (Luke 23:34).

We must remember that Jesus included everyone in these words—from Herod to Pilate, from the chief priests and scribes to the soldiers who scourged him.

And it was a blanket statement of love that has echoed across the centuries to you and me.

So, as Christian women, we can do no less than to follow Jesus' way of forgiveness, love, and compassion.

Letting Go of the Past

Forgetting what lies behind . . . , I press on. (Phil. 3:13–14, RSV)

The past is over and done with. To be free, we must learn how to let it go. And that usually means forgiving.

We often hear the phrase "Let go and let God." That means letting go of the past, especially situations or people we are holding to us in unforgiveness. For we have a prisoner and we are a jailer, both in bondage to each other, chained together with chains of unforgiveness.

The story of Lot and his wife is a good example of someone not letting go of the past. The Lord was merciful to Lot and his family by sending angels to take them to a safe place "lest they be consumed in the iniquity of the city of Sodom" (Gen. 19:15).

There was one warning given to the family: Do not look back. Press forward. Flee!

But we know what happened to Lot's wife. She looked back and was turned into a pillar of salt. Salt is a preservative. Lot's wife was attempting to hold on to the past. She didn't want to let go.

When we hold on to the garbage of the past we become stagnant. To clean out old grudges, guilts, angers, resentments, pet peeves, etc., isn't easy. Too often we are like Lot's wife, reluctant to give up the past, even though it wears us down and nearly kills us carrying it.

Why? Why do we cling so tightly to the past, even if we know it hurts us? Why don't we release it?

It takes courage to let the past go. And we are so buried in our habits that the pain of letting go of the familiar and facing the unknown is greater than the pain of carrying the comfortable "old shoes" of the past. Even if they are doing us harm.

So to break with the past we must affirm the courage to face ourselves. To handle the changes when they come. To be strong enough to look the past in the eye and forgive and say: "I don't need you anymore! Through Christ I am free. I welcome the new into my life—now!"

I have found that old thoughts, ideas, habits seem to have a life of their own and don't want to give us up. They want to stay and hold us in their prison. So the past goes easier if we forgive it and bless it and send it on its way. Fill your mind with your resources. Look forward to the new.

As you work freeing yourself from the past, you are rebuilding from within. And it isn't long before the outer changes. For it must change when you forgive and release—it is a law of God.

As We Forgive, So Are We Forgiven

Forgive us our debts, as we forgive our debtors. (Matt. 6:12)

When we forgive, we are working with the law of forgiveness and release—for our own salvation. This law is vital to our life— now, forever and throughout eternity.

For Jesus tells us we will be forgiven exactly how we forgive.

"But if ye forgive not men their trespasses, neither will your Father forgive your trespasses." (Matt. 6:15)

We find that judgment and condemnation work the same way.

"Judge not, that ye be not judged. For with what judgment ye judge, ye shall be judged: and with what measure ye mete, it shall be measured to you again." (Matt. 7:1–2)

> "Judge not, and ye shall not be judged:
> condemn not, and ye shall not be condemned:
> forgive, and ye shall be forgiven."
>
> (Luke 6:37)

So it seems that we set up our own criterion for forgiveness and judgment. It is awesome. But it also means that we have a "weapon" to change ourselves and others—even the world— through the laws of forgiveness and love.

Someone once said that if we would take time to sit down for a few minutes every evening before going to sleep and forgive— FORGIVE everyone in our life—it would change our world. So try it. Stop your activity, quietly affirming your resources. Then begin to forgive everyone—yourself, your husband, children, mother, father, sisters and brothers, neighbors, friends—anyone who comes to mind. Those in your community, government, state, country, and even world leaders.

When you work with this, *genuinely forgive*. Those of us who have tried this find that it takes about a month to understand this concept and break through. We find that the world is too much with us; we can't get through as we would like to at first. We are like the angel in Dan. 10:13 who had to work twenty-one days to get through to Daniel, and then he had to have help from the great archangel, Michael.

So don't let slow progress at first discourage you. You are making progress although you don't see it at first. Little by little you will see results in your outer life. Chains are being broken.

Forgiving When You Feel Crushed

Forgiving one another, just as God has forgiven you. (Eph. 4:32, TLB)

How difficult it is to forgive when you have been crushed or betrayed. When you have been let down and are disillusioned or disappointed. When you gave your faith and love and now there is nothing left but an aching heart and hurt.

This is the type of situation that puts a Christian to the test. And it takes everything within plus all our resources to win the battle.

Rose is a friend of mine who after middle age lived through such a traumatic and shocking time. For she found out that she had been betrayed by her husband of many years.

Rose had always been a hardworking and faithful wife. She went the extra mile in her marriage and reared the five children to be useful citizens. She loved her husband and felt they had a close relationship, although the last few years her job required working in the late evenings.

Then one day she found her husband had been unfaithful. It was an affair of several years. The shock and sorrow of the problem numbed her. For Rose was of the generation and life-style that believed in being faithful and married for life. It was difficult for her to come to terms with the problem.

Yet when Will, her husband, decided to return home and begged to be forgiven and taken back, she consented.

Rose honestly tried to forgive, but it was difficult for her. She couldn't release and let go.

One afternoon I visited her and noticed several clippings and books on adultery, broken marriages, etc., lying on the coffee table. Rose was keeping the sorrow alive by feeding it, continually thinking about it, even adding to it.

She was making both her husband and herself miserable. What more could he do? He had made a mistake and asked for forgiveness from both God and Rose and had tried in every way to show he was sincere.

Finally, one day Rose decided she had punished herself and Will enough. She knew she had to forgive. Her sanity and life depended upon it. And her salvation.

She knew she couldn't forgive by herself. Not humanly. So she asked the Holy Spirit to do the work of forgiveness for her until she could do it. Meanwhile she filled her mind with her resources, keeping her mind continually on God rather than the problem.

At first it was a moment-by-moment trial. She had to stand continually at the door of her mind to guide it in the way of forgiveness. She had to deal with questions that went like this: Why did this happen to me? How could he be so cruel? Then feelings of self-pity, torment, revenge, resentment, all the negatives kept knocking at her door. She had to say, "No!" a thousand times a day—"No!" to what she didn't want in her life. She had to learn to deny that the negatives no longer had a hold on her.

Finally the day came when she felt she could really forgive and relax her vigilance. She felt joy returning to her life and a renewal of love for Will.

At the age of seventy, Rose had won her victory.

Rose's way of forgiveness can be a lesson to us all. You can use it on any problem other than forgiveness—anything you want to change in your life.

1. Rose prayed that the Holy Spirit would help her. She knew she could not do it humanly. The hurt was too deep and she had felt completely betrayed. So she prayed that the Holy Spirit would help her become a loving, forgiving person. This was her true heartfelt desire. She set her will in this direction, even

though she didn't have the feeling that went with it. But she believed and had faith.

2. Rose prayed that the feeling of bitterness and the deep hurt she felt in the marrow of her bones would be replaced with God's love and understanding—and forgiveness.

3. Rose prayed that she could be forgiven and forgive herself for the feelings she harbored against herself, against her husband, even against God for allowing this to happen to her.

4. Rose prayed that not only would she be able to forgive but also to forget. That the incident would be wiped out of her heart and mind and that peace would replace it.

5. Rose prayed for her husband in his anguish and turmoil. That he be comforted and find peace also.

6. Finally, Rose prayed that their love would be reestablished as husband and wife. That their love would be stronger than before.

Rose won her victory because she held on—didn't give up. Today she says it is as though the problem never happened and their love is stronger than ever. And she smiles as she says, "Only through God could this come about!"

Practicing Instant Forgiveness

Do not let the sun go down on your anger. (Eph. 4:26, RSV)

The ultimate of forgiveness is to be able to forgive immediately, in an instant, at least the majority of the time.

It isn't easy, but the joy of instant forgiveness means that a hurt is taken care of immediately. There is no lingering disappointment or disillusionment and no grudge or resentment. So your lifeline to your resources is never clogged or cut.

The moment unforgiving thoughts come, we affirm God's grace. We quit looking for faults, criticizing or judging or condemning.

We feel cleansed, renewed, and joyful when we extend forgiveness to others. When we allow Christ to control our life, hurts are healed and we bless all situations with love.

It is a beautiful way to live.

RESOURCES

Since forgiveness is the center of Christianity, it is very important to understand how to forgive. Read and meditate on the following Scriptures, then use those at the end of Chapter 8 on love and Chapter 15 on joy. This will help reinforce forgiveness in your life.

WE KNOW THAT

The Son of man hath power on earth to forgive sins. (Mark 2:10)

FOR

Through Jesus the forgiveness of sins is proclaimed to you. (Acts 13:38, NIV)

SO

Do not judge, and you will not be judged. Do not condemn, and you will not be condemned. Forgive, and you will be forgiven. (Luke 6:37, NIV)

For if you forgive men when they sin against you,
your heavenly Father will also forgive you.
But if you do not forgive men their sins,
your Father will not forgive your sins. (Matt. 6:14–15, NIV)

AND WE LISTEN TO THIS GREAT PROMISE

Therefore I tell you, whatever you ask for in prayer, believe that you will receive it, and it will be yours. (Mark 11:24, NIV)

AND THE CONDITION THAT IS ATTACHED TO IT

And when you stand praying, if you hold anything against anyone, *forgive him,* so that your Father in heaven may forgive you your sins. (Mark 11:25, NIV)

SO

Be kind and compassionate to one another, forgiving each other, just as in Christ God forgave you. (Eph. 4:32, NIV)

AND SO WITH FORGIVENESS

Clothe yourselves with compassion, kindness, humility, gentleness and patience. (Col. 3:12, NIV)

AND

We were all baptized by one Spirit into one body—whether Jews or Greeks, slave or free. (I Cor. 12:13, NIV)

Where the Spirit of the Lord is, there is freedom. (II Cor. 3:17, RSV)

SO

Bear with each other and forgive whatever grievances you may have against one another.

Forgive as the Lord forgave you. (Col. 3:13, NIV)

AND JESUS IN THE PARABLE OF THE SERVANT WHO WOULDN'T FORGIVE TELLS US UNLESS WE FORGIVE OTHERS

This is how my heavenly Father will treat each of you unless you forgive your brother from your heart. (Matt. 18:35, NIV)

AND WHEN PETER ASKED HOW MANY TIMES SHALL I FORGIVE

Jesus answered, "I tell you, not seven times, but seventy-seven times." (Matt. 18:21–22, NIV)

SO WE KNOW THAT YOU ARE GOD

Kind and forgiving, O Lord, abounding in love to all who call to you. (Ps. 86:5, NIV)

A God ready to forgive, gracious and merciful. (Neh. 9:17, RSV)

AND SO WE PRAY

Forgive us our sins, for we also forgive everyone who sins against us. (Luke 11:4, NIV)

AND HE ANSWERS

Your sins are forgiven. (Matt. 9:2, NIV)

AND THE GREAT STATEMENT OF FORGIVENESS FROM THE CROSS

Father, forgive them; for they know not what they do. (Luke 23:34)

15
BANISHING DEPRESSION
The Need for Christian Joy

Why Not Live the Life of Joy?

Let them shout for joy, and be glad. (Ps. 35:27)

By now you have probably come to the conclusion, and rightly so, that I take Christian resources seriously. I feel that if a person is going to be a Christian, why be a halfhearted or lukewarm one? Why not go all the way?

Christian principles have an answer for every ill a person has on earth, whether mental, emotional, bodily, or spiritual. Why not use them?

And living your Christian resources means reaping the benefits. So now we come to an area where we will find out whether you are really partaking of the banquet table of Christianity, or whether you are still walking about, looking and yearning, or perhaps just nibbling a bit here and there.

The question is: Do you have joy in your life, the joy of the Lord? Do you have joy in your life *regardless of circumstances?*

Now I am not talking about a superficial happiness or a giggling gaiety but a deep abiding joy that bubbles out of you, giving you a feeling of specialness as a child of the King, a feeling that everything is A-O.K. regardless of what is going on about you.

This is the kind of joy a Christian woman should have.

Let's learn about it.

The Zoe Life of Joy

I am come that they might have life, and that they might have it more abundantly. (John 10:10)

Remember our theme verse of the abundant life? The Greek word used in this promise where Jesus tells us what kind of life he came to bring is the word *zoe*.

The Zoe kind of life is not the ordinary life.

It is the life of vitality, animation, and vigor. It is the life of rich and unfailing exuberance, absolute fullness, the emphatically illumined life.

It is the Christ life, as expressed by Jesus.

I don't believe we can live the Zoe life without understanding the joy of the Lord. The following Scriptures illustrate the special quality of the Zoe type of life:

"For as the Father hath life *(zoe)* in himself; so hath he given to the Son to have life *(zoe)* in himself." (John 5:26)

Also:

"In him was life *(zoe)*; and the life *(zoe)* was the light of men." (John 1:4)

This shows the joy, the nature of God, the life that we have within us. Proverbs says it this way: "The spirit of man is the candle of the LORD" (Prov. 20:27).

So having the "life abundantly" that Jesus was talking about, the Zoe kind of life, is a special gift for a Christian. And the Zoe kind of life is full of joy.

Open Your Life to Joy

Ask, and ye shall receive, that your joy may be full. (John 16:24)

Why not open your life to joy? There isn't a single one of us who doesn't want to be happy—and joyful. There isn't one of us who doesn't want to have the rewards of the Kingdom, including the life of joy.

Then why don't we?

It is simply that old habits are stronger than the desire for the new. It takes many more muscles to frown than to smile. But you see more frowns than smiles. We are so comfortable with the negative. A field not taken care of and tilled soon turns to weeds.

Oh, you say, but you don't know my problems. I'm sick and have financial responsibilities; I'm depressed and discouraged. What do I have to be joyful about? Look at all the troubles I have. Look at all the pain I'm in.

Let me tell you right now, I understand. I have compassion and empathy, because I have been there.

But I have also learned that until you set your mind and will toward joy—allow the joy of the Lord to enter your life—you will be what I call a limping Christian, one who reads and talks more about the banquet table than eats and enjoys. If your religion is about as happy as a sour pickle, you have missed the essence of your resources.

Depression is one of the scourges of today's woman. Everyone at one time or another becomes depressed. But many people stay depressed for much too long. (I'm not talking about a problem of depression that needs medication.)

Several years ago I did quite a bit of counseling and held my Joy of Living Seminars. During that time I noticed depression was rampant, even among committed believers. Some had simply slipped into bad habit patterns, others accepted depression as a part of their life, still others didn't know how to get out of it.

Depression can be turned into joy. Since I have only one chapter to talk about it, we can only cover the high points. If you go through the day dragging, depressed, gloomy, and dark, no matter what you know or what you have, it doesn't mean anything. For you can't enjoy it.

I am writing from experience. For years depression was always nipping at my heels, because I made myself miserable. I felt as if I had been given the earth-shattering job of being the world's referee. And if I wasn't worrying, I wondered why I wasn't worrying. I found that I had two foundational beliefs that ruled my life. One was that if I worried enough, that would keep negative things from happening. I was paying some sort of dues. The second was that my self-image was dark. I felt that I didn't deserve happiness.

Then one day the full meaning of Jesus' words pierced my soul. I thought, What would really happen if I believed? If Jesus' words of the abundant life were true? If I took his words as my credo rather than my continual worrisome outlook?

And when I looked about in my life to find what was reinforcing my depressive outlook, it was everything from my habits to my church. Even Sunday mornings were all variations on the theme, What if we died before next Sunday? It took me all week to get my spirits up, and then it was Sunday again.

I decided to break the worry habit. I changed many things in my life (including my church). I found that Jesus was the overcomer, that was what he wanted for us. And you don't overcome while in depression.

It took much will and effort to retrain my mind. I still must be vigilant, stand guard at the door of my mind. I have learned there is great power in our ability to say no! It is as important as saying yes to what we do want.

So stir up your joy and enthusiasm. Success motivators say there is nothing more important than joy and enthusiasm. Your attitude is important in everything you do in life.

Open your life to joy.

Act joyful and you will be joyful was a secret I learned. Act out an emotion and the feeling will follow. We do this all the time in the negative, so why not do it in the positive and enjoy life?

Set your heart and mind in the direction of joy. There is an inner strength in joy that is spiritual and pure, for joy comes from an inner reservoir of God's goodness.

The Joy of the Lord

The joy of the LORD is your strength. (Neh. 8:10)

If you have the joy of the Lord, you have learned:

1. *Not to Put Off Your Joy*
Now is the time for joy. One of the greatest of joy robbers is excuses we make. Often we will say we will be happy and joyful when we get married (or divorced), when we have that special job, when we have a child, when the kids are grown, when we buy a house, when our mortgage gets paid off, when our ship comes in.

If you continue with this type of thinking, you will postpone your joy forever. You know the benefits of the Kingdom. Take a stand.

If you don't, you are living one of the greatest lies of the adversary. The next step is blaming circumstances for your unhappiness.

You can take charge of your life and have joy. You determine your happiness. You can have joy in the midst of difficulties, in spite of conditions.

2. To Make Your Imagination Work for You

If you have joy in your life, you have learned to harness your imagination and make it work for you. You make it produce pictures of what you want in your life, rather than what you don't want.

Learn to keep your imagination under control. You keep it from bothering you with mistakes from the past, concerns of the future, toxic worries, and unfounded fears.

Put your imagination in a joy gear. Keep it working for you in the positive. It is a tremendous tool for good.

3. To Make the Battle the Lord's

There is a time to release and make the battle the Lord's. Let your worries go and turn your projects over to God. You quit controlling or manipulating in an unhealthy manner. Frustration comes from trying to get others to do it your way. Release them now.

4. To Experience Mountaintops and Valleys

There are mountaintop experiences and then there are valley experiences. With the joy of the Lord even your valley experiences will be good.

I love to travel on mountain roads. The Blue Ridge Parkway in the Great Smoky Mountains of North Carolina is probably my favorite drive in all the world.

And when we are driving on the crest and looking down at the beautiful villages in the valleys, we wonder why in the spiritual realm valleys don't have a better reputation.

There is no doubt about it, in the valleys come the great lessons of life. But what we experienced on the mountaintop helps us in

175

the valleys. We can't stay on the mountaintop forever, our spiritual wattage would be burned out.

But in the valleys our resources are no less than they were on the mountaintop.

So what is the great difference?

In the valley our vision is limited, we have to go on faith. On the mountaintop we see, we understand, we are spiritually in tune. We know! We have joy!

But as we travel in the valley on faith, even though our view is stunted, we also know. In the valley no matter how deep—sometimes we don't even see the sun till midmorning—yet we have joy. We have our resources and we know. And that brings joy into our life, no matter where we are.

5. *To Begin Your Day with Your Resources*

If you begin your day with your resources and you affirm joy, that is what your day will bring. Set your mind and will toward joy. Allow this Scripture to set the tone of your day:

"This is the day which the LORD hath made; we will rejoice and be glad in it" (Ps. 118:24).

You are the carrier of your joy. You decide. By now you know how much authority God has given you. So when I say our joy is up to us, you know what I mean.

6. *To Use Your Resources*

If you put the resources of God as used in this book into operation in your life, it will lead to joy. For joy and happiness are byproducts of LIVING and UNDERSTANDING God's resources.

God's resources are given for you. Use them.

My Clothesline of Joy

Many things come into our life that attempt to make us miserable and rob us of joy.

Some sneak into our life on cat's feet. Others come thundering like a herd of elephants. Still others come in nit-picking and biting like swarms of mosquitoes or gnats, buzzing and bothering us. They all can take away our Christian poise and joy. And they can keep us busy in the morass of doubt and indecision, for once we give the negative a toehold, trouble follows.

176

So I have developed what I call my Joy Clothesline. I am sure it is not original but it serves its purpose, and those whom I have shared it with said it made great changes in their lives. For it is a technique to win over the enemy. And it works.

I visualize my clothesline as a strong firm one with an old-fashioned cord that won't snag or sag. It is tight and straight and completely in the Sonlight. For on this clothesline I will hang anything that attempts to rob me of Christian joy.

I created this clothesline at first to hang up my religious doubts. As a researcher and a pilgrim on the way looking for a faith, I had gathered over six thousand books in my personal library. (Even though the house sags, my husband is tolerant.)

As I studied about religions of the world, many had such conflicting views that I hung them on my clothesline "awaiting further light."

And as the years went by I found many of the items on my clothesline were disappearing. Christianity wiped them out. The more I studied, the more I found that the religion brought to earth by Jesus Christ was the True Light.

So I began to use my clothesline for anything that robbed me of joy, and most of the time I found that the Sonlight dissolved it. Whether it was questions that bothered philosophers for centuries, for which no one has found an answer, or conflicts or worries of the daily life.

Use this clothesline and don't allow questions or conflicts to rob you of vital energy. Hang them up and you will find, in the majority of cases, the Holy Spirit will one day give you a flash of insight—just the answer for you.

One time I shared the concept of my clothesline—a little timidly, I admit—with a prominent pastor. I felt somewhat shy and backward wondering if he would think I was a little teched.

But he just laughed. "Hey," he said. "That's much more sophisticated than what I use." Then he went on to explain: "I've got a terrible temper. Have had it most of my life. And no matter what I tried, it kept getting the best of me. One day I realized I just couldn't go on any longer. A member of my congregation did something so unjust, so abusive—well, you know what I mean. So suddenly the picture of my mama's old galvanized washtub came into my mind. The way she picked us up and dunked us. So I picked up my temper and feelings I held about this man by the scruff of the neck and dunked them in Mama's bent-up tub and baptized them with love. It worked. I found I could transmute my negative emotions this way. They weren't buried but transmuted. And I was free."

Then he added with a twinkle: "Sometimes I have to jump into that old tub myself. And it always does me good. I come out feeling cleansed and full of love and joy."

So whether you use clothesline or tub or whatever, cleansing with love always equals joy.

RESOURCES

One of the greatest benefits about our resources is the great and wonderful power of joy. There will be many times in your life when sadness or depression or just plain "tiredness" attempts to enter your life.

Chase these negatives away with "joy power." Joy is invigoration. It infuses you with a special enthusiasm and love like nothing else will, except for praise. So put joy and praise resources together, for it is like fueling up with the highest octane power.

Joy is yours. It is given to you. It is one of the greatest of strengths for the overcomers of the Kingdom.

Use it today.

WE KNOW

The joy of the LORD is our strength. (Neh. 8:10)

AND

A happy heart is good medicine and a cheerful mind works
healing, but a broken spirit dries the bones. (Prov. 17:22)

ALSO

A merry heart maketh a cheerful countenance. (Prov. 15:13)

FURTHERMORE

A merry heart hath a continual feast. (Prov. 15:15)

AND SO BELIEVING IN GOD, OUR FATHER, WE CAN SAY

Thou wilt show me the path of life: in thy presence is fulness
of joy; at thy right hand there are pleasures for evermore. (Ps.
16:11)

SO

I will be glad and rejoice in thy mercy. (Ps. 31:7)

ALSO
Let the heavens rejoice, and let the earth be glad; Let the sea roar, and the fulness thereof. Let the field be joyful, and all that is therein: Then shall all the trees of the wood rejoice. (Ps. 96:11–12)
THEN
I went with them to the house of God, with the voice of joy and praise. (Ps. 42:4)

Then will I go unto the altar of God, unto God my exceeding joy:
Yea, upon the harp will I praise thee, O God my God. (Ps. 43:4)
AND THAT UPHOLDS ME WHEN I AM IN A VALLEY OF LIFE, FOR
Weeping may endure for a night, but joy cometh in the morning. (Ps. 30:5)

They shall obtain joy and gladness, and sorrow and sighing shall flee away. (Isa. 35:10)
FOR YOU WILL
Restore unto me the joy of thy salvation; and uphold me with thy free Spirit. (Ps. 51:12)
AND YOU TELL US TO
Enter thou into the joy of thy lord. (Matt. 25:21)

Ask, and ye shall receive, that your joy may be full. (John 16:24)
AND REGARDLESS OF CIRCUMSTANCES WE
Count it all joy. (James 1:2)
FOR WE KNOW WE SHALL HAVE
The voice of joy, and the voice of gladness. (Jer. 33:11)
AND WE ARE ALSO TOLD THAT
Your joy no man taketh from you. (John 16:22)
AND WE REJOICE BECAUSE OF THE BIRTH OF THE ONE WHO FREED US AND OVERCAME FOR US AND LED US TO JOY
When they saw the star, they rejoiced with exceeding great joy. (Matt. 2:10)
AND THE ANGEL SAID
Fear not: for, behold, I bring you good tidings of great joy, which shall be to all people. (Luke 2:10)

179

And there shall be joy and gladness; and many shall rejoice at his birth. (Luke 1:14)

AND SO AT THE BIRTH OF JESUS CHRIST WE

Rejoice with joy unspeakable and full of glory. (I Peter 1:8)

FOR HE CAME SO

That your joy may be full. (I John 1:4)

SO WE SAY

O let the nations be glad and sing for joy. (Ps. 67:4)

Let them shout for joy, and be glad. (Ps. 35:27)

And my soul shall be joyful in the LORD. (Ps. 35:9)

SO EVERY MORNING I WILL SAY

This is the day which the LORD hath made; we will rejoice and be glad in it. (Ps. 118:24)

AND WE HAVE BEEN

Anointed with the oil of gladness. (Ps. 45:7)

AND SO WITH JOY

My cup runneth over. (Ps. 23:5)

16
NOW IS THE TIME

The Need to Use Time Wisely

God's Time and Our Time

With the Lord a day is like a thousand years, and a thousand years are like a day. (II Peter 3:8, NIV)

We have divided time into years, days, hours, minutes—and moments. This is done by the rotation and travel of the earth. If we measure our time against God's time, as in the above Scripture, our life on earth could be called but a parenthesis in eternity. For it must be just a flicker of the eyelash of God.

God's time is eternity—and more. When we begin thinking of the "eternal now" it makes God's time practically beyond our comprehension.

But there is great comfort in knowing that God is timeless and changeless. He is the same yesterday, today, and tomorrow (Heb. 13:8). He tells us that he is the Lord who changes not (Mal. 3:6). He is from everlasting to everlasting (Ps. 90:2). And one of his titles is "the everlasting Father" (Isa. 9:6).

So that means that—God is! He always has been and always will be.

Living in the Now

Behold, now is the accepted time; Behold, now is the day of salvation. (II Cor. 6:2)

I had heard about "living in the now," living each moment

fully and joyfully, savoring it and enjoying it. But I evidently didn't understand the concept, for I was still fussing and fuming about time. I was a committed believer in other areas of my life, but the secret of making time work for me had escaped me.

In fact, I was constantly battling the hours of the day, affirming negatively that "I don't have enough time!" My nerves were on edge, tensions mounted, and in my war with time—I lost.

Then one day I realized what was wrong. I wasn't using my resources to begin my day. I found that I had to affirm what I wanted early in the morning—and throughout my day. And give thanks for it.

So I began to affirm order, strength, peace, wisdom for my day. I visualized what I desired. For wasn't this "the day which the LORD hath made; we will rejoice and be glad in it" (Ps. 118:24)?

Finally, after several months, I began to see results—by how I felt at the *end* of the day. I found that I had accomplished more, was in better spirits with less exhaustion, and had less of a feeling of being harassed and harried by time.

So I found that if my day was hemmed in prayer, it was less likely to unravel.

What's Your Hurry?

Rest in the LORD, and wait patiently for him. (Ps. 37:7)

Truly my soul waiteth upon God: from him cometh my salvation. (Ps. 62:1)

Did you know that you really have all the time in the world? So what's your hurry?

We have found that we are what we think and believe. The same holds true of what we believe about time. Time used wisely—without rushing, without allowing the clamor of the world to interfere—makes us much more productive.

Try this. When you feel the most rushed, when you are frazzled, when things seem their most frantic, when everything is upset, including you—STOP!

Stop for a minute. Stop and "be still, and know that I am God" (Ps. 46:10).

Breathe deeply and relax. I like to use favorite Scriptures at this time. One is:

182

"But they that wait upon the LORD shall renew their strength;
they shall mount up with wings as eagles;
they shall run, and not be weary; and
they shall walk, and not faint."

(Isa. 40:31)

Use any of your resources that would be helpful. It takes no more than a minute to relax and affirm strength and joy. It changes the atmosphere by breaking the spell of frantic action and squirrel-caging thought.

So slow down and save time.

The Grazing Principle

Whatsoever thy hand findeth to do, do it with thy might. (Eccl. 9:10)

There is a principle that can help you stretch time by making you more productive.

Have you ever watched cattle in a pasture grazing? It is an interesting experiment. I love to sit under the cottonwood trees in the grove and watch them eat. They don't run from one end of a field to another, nibbling a little here and a bit there and grabbing a clump of grass that looks good.

No, they work systematically, cropping off the grass as it comes before them. They eat the grass within the reach of their nose, even though they see a richer stand of grass farther on.

We can take a lesson from this principle. It helps us to be more productive by doing the task at hand "with all our might."

It also helps us answer the question, What is the will of God for me? Some people get all out of kilter searching for what God wants them to *do*. The following explains it:

> You asked me what is the will of God
> And I will answer true.
> It's the nearest thing that should be done
> That God can do through you.

God's will for you isn't complex. It always begins with the nearest thing at hand to do. Then it can lead to greater things.

183

The Secret of Time Management

My chosen shall long enjoy the work of their hands. (Isa. 65:22, RSV)

Sometime ago I had to make a study of time management. As I studied book after book, I found that nearly all the experts had the same "secret." It was often covered up with a lot of financial world jargon, but it all came out the same.

And this secret has been around for years. In fact, there is a story that happened around the turn of the century. Charles Schwab, president of Bethlehem Steel, asked a time management expert to give him a way to increase production, to make the plant more efficient in every way.

The expert, a Mr. Lee, wrote down a formula for Mr. Schwab and said: "Try this for several months. After that time you can pay me what you think it is worth!"

Several months later Mr. Schwab sent Mr. Lee a check for twenty-five thousand dollars!

Since that time no one has come up with a better formula. It will work for you if you are president of a corporation, business manager of a hospital, owner of a pet shop or a bakery, or manager of a household.

This is the formula:

1. Make a list of things that need to be done.
2. Arrange them according to priority.
3. Do them one by one.

Rose Kennedy used to have a quaint habit of pinning notes of things to be done on the bodice of her dress. With a house full of children, servants, friends, and neighbors, there was always much to do. So she would begin the day covered with slips of paper, pinned on upside down so she could read them. She said sometimes she felt like a fluttering scarecrow, but as the day went by, she would tear them off according to their priority.

So whether you write your lists on a clipboard or the back of an envelope, or pin them on your dress, this simple formula works.

You Can Begin Again

Behold, I make all things new. (Rev. 21:5)

Old things are passed away; behold, all things are become new. (II Cor. 5:17)

One of the most wonderful benefits of your Christian resources is that you can begin again. Time never runs out. It is never too late.

I received a call from Elaine a few months ago. She had been a believer in the past but through the years had gotten away from her resources.

Now she told me she had become involved with the husband of her best friend. Before long two marriages were wrecked, one with two children and the other with three.

Elaine had now come to her senses and broken with the man and wanted to repair the damage that she had done to her marriage. But her husband didn't want her back.

So she was depressed, full of pessimism and fears and doubts. And she kept repeating, "It's too late, it's too late!"

I told her God cared about her. Right now. This moment. And she could begin again. It is never too late. God was still in the forgiving business, and he would give her the strength and courage to do what she must.

After we had talked awhile she finally was convinced that God would forgive her and that she could begin again. She realized that she had to work hard. It wouldn't be easy. But perhaps in time her family would be together again. Elaine was willing to face the challenge.

As the days went by, God was with Elaine and sustained her through some difficult times. She is seeing her husband again and he realizes he is talking to a different Elaine. The old Elaine is no more. She is a new person and there is hope for their marriage to begin again.

You can begin again. God will see you through. These are not just words I am writing. There is power in the love of God. He has the ways and the means that we don't understand.

Have faith and it will work for you. No matter what has

happened in the past. God will forgive and see you through. Cling to your resources and keep the line open.

Time Robbers

Reverence for God adds hours to each day. (Prov. 10:27, TLB)

There are many time robbers in our life. Some of those I have found in my own life are:

1. *Disorder*
"Set thine house in order." (Isa. 38:1)
"Let all things be done decently and in order." (I Cor. 14:40)
The poet tells us that order is heaven's first law. It certainly seems that way, for without order in our life we cannot be productive. Make lists of things to change, throw out, straighten up, give away, clean up, or redo.

2. *Indecision and Procrastination*
"He becometh poor that dealeth with a slack hand: but the hand of the diligent maketh rich." (Prov. 10:4)
"Commit your work to the Lord, then it will succeed." (Prov. 16:3, TLB)
Why put off until tomorrow what you can do today? Indecision and procrastination can be a habit. I have found that when I use my resources for courage and self-image, disliked tasks are easier done.

3. *Making Life Too Complex*
"We should make plans—counting on God to direct us." (Prov. 16:9, TLB)
Your life can be made a lot easier and you can save much time if you simplify. Change your life by the elimination of things that are unnecessary. You will find simplifying will change the quality of your life for the better.

4. *Playing Superwoman*
"It is better to have self-control than to control an army." (Prov. 16:32, TLB)
"Pride goes before destruction." (Prov. 16:18, TLB)

When we play superwoman, whether in the home or the office, we end up working ourselves into a frazzle.

Learn to delegate authority and check what false responsibility you are carrying. Is it really your job? Is it really your business?

Abdicate your throne. Your false ego has ruled you long enough.

5. *Living Yesterday, Today, and Tomorrow All at Once*

"God is not the author of confusion, but of peace." (I Cor. 14:33)

"Determination to be wise is the first step toward becoming wise!" (Prov. 4:7, TLB)

Trying to live yesterday, today, and tomorrow all at once in a jumble can keep you in a state of confusion and loses you much time.

Yesterday is a canceled check, tomorrow is a promissory note— so today is all you have. When you learn to live one day at a time, you find that your days are richer, more appreciated, and you savor life in a way as never before.

RESOURCES

Time is elusive. It is only when you have faith that time works for you. The stronger you are in faith and using your resources, the better time treats you. And the more productive you become.

WE KNOW

To every thing there is a season, and a time to every purpose under the heaven. (Eccl. 3:1)

FOR

The LORD knoweth the days of the upright: and their inheritance shall be for ever. (Ps. 37:18)

You have made my days a mere handbreath; the span of my years is as nothing before you.

Each man's life is but a breath. (Ps. 39:5, NIV)

SO IT IS WISE TO

Wait for the LORD and keep his way. (Ps. 37:34, NIV)

FOR WE KNOW

He hath made every thing beautiful in his time. (Eccl. 3:11)

The heavens declare the glory of God; the skies proclaim the work of his hands. (Ps. 19:1, NIV)

AND

The law of the LORD is perfect, reviving the soul.
The statutes of the LORD are trustworthy, making wise the simple. (Ps. 19:7, NIV)

The path of the righteous is like the first gleam of dawn, shining ever brighter till the full light of day. (Prov. 4:18, NIV)

AND WE ARE TOLD

Do not forget this one thing, dear friends: With the Lord a day is like a thousand years, and a thousand years are like a day. (II Peter 3:8, NIV)

AND THEN WE ARE TOLD

I am the LORD, I change not. (Mal. 3:6)

Jesus Christ is the same yesterday and today and for ever. (Heb. 13:8, RSV)

AND WE REPLY

From everlasting to everlasting, thou art God. (Ps. 90:2)

AND WE ARE GIVEN THIS PROMISE

The reverent and worshipful fear of the Lord prolongs one's days. (Prov. 10:27, AMP)

AND WE KNOW

This day is a day of good tidings. (II Kings 7:9)

FOR

Every good gift and every perfect gift is from above, and cometh down from the Father of lights, with whom is no variableness, neither shadow of turning. (James 1:17)

SO WITH JOY AND THANKSGIVING WE KNOW

This is the day which the LORD hath made; we will rejoice and be glad in it. (Ps. 118:24)

AND WE ARE TOLD

Do not worry or be anxious about tomorrow, for tomorrow will have worries and anxieties of its own. Sufficient for each day is its own trouble. (Matt. 6:34, AMP)

And which of you by worrying and being anxious can add one unit of measure [cubit] to his stature or to the span of his life? (Matt. 6:27, AMP)

SO REMEMBER THIS PROMISE

I will go before thee, and make the crooked places straight. (Isa. 45:2)

17
AGE IS A STATE OF MIND

The Need to Enjoy Each Stage of Life

Life: God's Gift to Us

Mine age is as nothing before thee. (Ps. 39:5)

Life is God's gift to us. It is to be enjoyed, savored, and we give thanks for it.

Age is a state of mind, for we have our roots in eternity. For as a child of God, we are ageless. Our life on earth is but a tiny particle of eternity, of the everlasting.

So we can be eternally young, no matter what stage of life we are living. Each period of life can bring its own rewards, with much excitement if we look for it and recognize it.

We know that as children of God on earth we are loved and cherished. Each of us is an individual who is completely unique. And we know that God knows us so well that the hair on our head is numbered (Luke 12:7).

We are given a number of years to love and grow and we find that we can make a contribution in every stage of life. Nothing is ever wasted, in our spirit or in our experience. It is all grist for the mill of living, loving, and learning.

We are as a tree, flourishing as long as its tap root is centered in our Source. We thrive as long as we don't cut off our connection. And as we continually reach out to new experiences—to life and love and growth—we find that years do not matter. For God is continually expressing himself through us. We are his handiwork and who else but us does he have?

So as a child of God, no matter what your age, you are blessed.

Something good is happening to you no matter what stage of life you are in. Look for it and live life to the fullest. Live abundantly!

The Stages of Life

How excellent is thy loving-kindness, O God! Therefore the children of man put their trust under the shadow of thy wings. (Ps. 36:7)

Each stage of life carries its own unique qualities. It has its own excitement of growth—of being.

1. *The Formative Years: 0–18*
"For thou art my hope, O Lord GOD: thou art my trust from my youth." (Ps. 71:5)
These are the years we spend under the guidance of our parents. During this time we are shaped and molded by our mother and father, teachers and friends. This is the period where our God-given potentials and our environment meet. We are like rough stones that are taken and polished into diamonds with many facets.

2. *The Early Years: 18–40*
"O God, thou hast taught me from my youth: and hitherto have I declared thy wondrous works." (Ps. 71:17)
This is the time when the world looks the most fresh and lovely to us. We think we can do anything—and we can. We have the enthusiasm of youth, we have not become worn or jaded in our thinking. We are encouraged, because we see possibilities on every hand. We look for ways to change situations and people.
Children are given to us during these years because they need the energy and stimulation of the young mother. Our children are in the formative stage during this time and they need our nurturing and Christian training.
This is the time of great energy and the years to enjoy new directions—new vistas. These are the take-charge years.

3. *The Middle Years: 40–65*
"Commit thy works unto the LORD, and thy thoughts shall be established." (Prov. 16:3)

190

Now we come to the most productive years. We have learned from the early years and have the wisdom that is necessary to work toward our goals. We are steady, firm, and determined. The keywords for these years are work and productivity.

These are the best years for the career-minded woman. The children are grown and she can pursue goals. During these years many women resurrect a dream and work toward success.

4. *The Latter Years: 65 and Beyond*

"I have been young, and now am old; yet have I not seen the righteous forsaken. . . . He is ever merciful." (Ps. 37:25–26)

Now, if you really understand your Source, you are looking forward to new beginnings. It could be retirement—to greater things. For there is a new dream ahead, tempered by wisdom. For in living through the years, you now have learned how to be selective about what you wish to do. And the years have taught you what you can do effectively.

You know that keeping busy—reaching out—is the key during these years. For statistics show that those who live the longest always have goals before them: a short-term goal that is easy to fulfill and a long-term goal for the future.

As the psalmist says: young or old, yet God will never forsake us. He is ever merciful and will answer us if we call upon him. That is a promise.

Success Is Possible at Any Age

Remember now thy Creator in the days of thy youth. (Eccl. 12:1)

They shall still bring forth fruit in old age. (Ps. 92:14)

Success can be yours at any age. For it is not the age that brings success, but the strong dream and desire.

When we think of success late in life we think of Grandma Moses, who began painting after the age of seventy and who was still turning out wonderful work at nearly one hundred.

We think of Corrie ten Boom, who was still a "tramp for the Lord" at nearly eighty. And Rose Kennedy, who just passed her ninety-third birthday! And how about Mrs. Norman Vincent Peale, who still works beside her husband, counseling and writing, and is past seventy. Then we know of people in their mature years like Dale Evans, Marjorie Holmes, and Eugenia Price, who are turning out work that is better than ever.

Success is possible at any age!

The Best Years

So teach us to number our days, that we may apply our hearts unto wisdom. (Ps. 90:12)

What are the best years? Fifteen? Thirty-five? Fifty-five? How about sixty, seventy, eighty, or ninety?

We know that the best years are the years you are living—NOW! Whatever your age.

So enjoy them. If you are a Christian with the joy of the Lord within you, you are an overcomer. So any age is the best age for you. Savor and live life to the fullest!

God can help you turn the most trying times about. You will find that you can take a lemon and make a sparkling, clear glass of yellow lemonade!

The following four friends have done just that. At every age they, by practicing their resources, turned what was a challenge into a triumph!

1. Sabrina, in her twenties, had an illness that kept her housebound. At first she chafed at the bit, becoming unhappy and resentful. Then one day she learned about her resources and began to use them in earnest. Soon she was led to look for something special that God had planned for her so she opened her mind to opportunities. Not long after, she was reading a children's book when the thought came to her that she could write one. Even a better one! Now she writes and illustrates books for preschoolers. Her favorite Scripture is:

"Then Jesus told them, 'Truly, if you have faith, and don't doubt, you can do things like this and much more. You can even say to this Mount of Olives, "Move over into the ocean," and it will. You can get anything—*anything* you ask for in prayer—if you believe.'" (Matt. 21:21–22, TLB)

2. My friend Abby is in her early thirties and what she desired

192

most in the world was to have children. But she and Ted were married ten years and now tests showed there were to be no children. At first it was a disappointment and brought an ache and longing to her heart. But it soon turned to joy when she and Ted had the opportunity to adopt two youngsters who desperately needed a home and family. Now their household rings with joy.

Abby's favorite Scripture is:

"Delight yourself in the LORD and he will give you the desires of your heart." (Ps. 37:4, NIV)

3. Carla is a widow in her forties with three teenagers, fifteen, sixteen, and seventeen. They nearly overwhelmed her. When she found out that they were all involved in drugs, Carla thought it was the end.

Then she remembered her resources and began to believe that God had a right answer to the situation. So Carla sat down with her Bible and claimed the promises and visualized her children whole and happy for three twenty-minute periods a day. She saw them laughing and working, free from drugs. She visualized Jesus with his arms around each child, guiding, gently leading each one in the right direction. And she gave thanks for it. For it was so in her spirit and she knew it would manifest itself so in the outer world.

Bit by bit the children straightened out through the Palmer Drug Abuse program. Now Carla and her three children all work in the program helping others to get off drugs.

When I asked Carla what her favorite verse was, she said, "All of them!" For she explained that she lived and breathed the Scriptures the nineteen months she prayed and visualized her children whole and productive and happy. And she loves the concept of seeing Jesus as the good shepherd, loving and caring for his lambs.

"I am the good shepherd, and know my sheep." (John 10:14)

"The LORD is my shepherd; I shall not want." (Ps. 23:1)

Then she added that without Matt. 11:28–30 she would have gone under. On days when the situation was quite rough and she had to go strictly on faith, she would do exactly what these Scriptures told her to do.

"Come unto me, all ye that labor and are heavy laden, and I will give you rest. Take my yoke upon you, and learn of me; for

I am meek and lowly in heart: and ye shall find rest unto your souls. For my yoke is easy, and my burden is light." (Matt. 11:28–30)

4. Libby's husband, Cal, had a heart attack. They were both in their early seventies and through the years they had wandered from their Source. Now, through the recovery period, they had found their way back. The spiritual help and comfort they received when they turned to God is everything to them. They are happier now than they have ever been. And they no longer fear the future.

Libby and Cal have read the Bible through several times and constantly find Scriptures that they learn from. So they have many favorites, but any Scripture that tells about the glory and wonder of God is a favorite! For they cannot tell of his praises enough.

"Oh, what a wonderful God we have! How great are his wisdom and knowledge and riches! How impossible it is for us to understand his decisions and his methods! For who among us can know the mind of the Lord? Who knows enough to be his counselor and guide? . . . For everything comes from God alone. Everything lives by his power, and everything is for his glory. To him be glory evermore." (Rom. 11:33–34, 36, TLB)

So you see, even through adversity the best years are *now!* No matter what the circumstances. We can learn and grow and be happy where we are, this moment.

So find the good in your life NOW. Sometimes it is momentarily covered up by circumstances. But God's good will shine through if you look for it. In every challenge, no matter what your age, there is a seed for good.

The best years are now!

RESOURCES

We know that each stage of life carries its own rewards. Christian women are overcomers no matter what their age. And of primary importance is your self-image. So the following resources can be combined with those in Chapter 1 to show how special, as a child of God, you really are!

AS WE BEGIN IN YOUTH WE ARE TOLD

Let no man despise thy youth. (I Tim. 4:12)

For thou art my hope, O Lord GOD: thou art my trust from my youth. (Ps. 71:5)

O God, thou hast taught me from my youth: and hitherto have I declared thy wondrous works. (Ps. 71:17)

SO I WILL

Remember now thy Creator in the days of thy youth. (Eccl. 12:1)

AND THEN AS WE MOVE ALONG IN LIFE

We spend our years as a tale that is told. (Ps. 90:9)

FOR WE REALIZE

Mine age is as nothing before thee. (Ps. 39:5)

SO WE ASK GOD TO

Teach us to number our days, that we may apply our hearts unto wisdom. (Ps. 90:12)

AND THEN AS THE YEARS PASS WE FIND

The hoary head is a crown of glory. (Prov. 16:31)

AND WE KNOW

They shall still bring forth fruit in old age. (Ps. 92:14)

AND WE COMPARE THE LATTER YEARS TO FINE WINE

No man also having drunk old wine straightway desireth new; for he saith, The old is better. (Luke 5:39)

AND OFTEN WE FIND AS DID JOB

So the Lord blessed Job at the end of his life more than at the beginning. (Job 42:12, TLB)

AND FINALLY WE HAVE THESE PROMISES

Forget not my law; but let thine heart keep my commandments:

for length of days, and long life, and peace, shall they add to thee. (Prov. 3:1–2)

AND

The fear of the LORD is the beginning of wisdom: and the knowledge of the Holy is understanding.

For by me thy days shall be multiplied, and the years of thy life shall be increased. (Prov. 9:10–11)

AND FINALLY THE GREAT PROMISE IN ONE OF THE TEN COMMANDMENTS

Honor thy father and thy mother, as the LORD thy God commanded thee; that thy days may be prolonged, and that it may go well with thee. (Deut. 5:16)

18

THE WHOLE WOMAN

Body, Mind, and Spirit

The Wonderful You!

I praise you because I am fearfully and wonderfully made. (Ps. 139:14, NIV)

How wonderful we are! We are made in the image and likeness of God—a child of the King and an inheritor of the Kingdom. And as a three-part individual with body, mind, and spirit, we worship a loving and sovereign God.

And as a child of God, we are, as the psalmist says, "fearfully and wonderfully made." For we are spiritual beings living on earth in a body with a mind that is capable of choice and a spirit that is eternally linked to our Source.

The Body

Know ye not that ye are the temple of God, and that the Spirit of God dwelleth in you? (I Cor. 3:16)

We marvel at the intricacies of our body.

And our body is the dwelling place of the Spirit of God. So it is important that we take excellent care of our body, through the right food, exercise, and attitude.

I have found that when I bless and give thanks for my body that it responds with good health. I bless and give thanks for my body from head to toe—brain, liver, intestines, bones, heart, blood vessels, stomach, lungs, kidneys, etc. I continually affirm that my body is doing its work in a perfect way.

For what we bless prospers and we are told:

"Beloved, I wish above all things that thou mayest prosper and be in health, even as thy soul prospereth" (III John 2).

This verse also shows how intertwined our body, mind, and spirit are. We must be in good balance to live the good life.

In analyzing the people who they say live the longest on earth, the Hunza people of the Himalayas, the people of the mountains of South Russia, and the people of the mountains of Ecuador, we find something interesting. We find the same pattern that is given to us today by the latest experts on nutrition, exercise, and attitude.

1. The mountain people eat sparingly, but enough to maintain good health and energy. Their diet consists of whole grains, vegetables, and fruits (especially apricots). They eat some fish and fowl but only eat animal protein two or three times a week.

This is consistent with what our experts say is a diet for good health today.

2. They drink mineral-laden but clear sparkling water from mountain streams. We are told to drink the healthiest water possible and at least eight glasses a day.

3. Living in the mountains the people walk up and down steep terrain daily, giving their legs a good workout. This corresponds with what the experts tell us, to exercise daily, if only a walk.

4. The mountain people have a good nature and a smiling serenity. They stay active with a feeling of being useful no matter what their age.

And their belief in a long life shows in the way they make their toasts with their native wines. Instead of saying "May you live to be a hundred!" as we do, they say:

"May you live to be three hundred years old!"

The Mind

For as he thinketh in his heart, so is he. (Prov. 23:7)

Keep thy heart with all diligence; for out of it are the issues of life. (Prov. 4:23)

Our mind is what makes us the people of the free will, able to choose this day whom we shall serve.

I have written this book to show why we should continually live in the Kingdom, why we should choose God. We know that Jesus came to free us spiritually and mentally from any limitation. And to do this we must continually keep this mind in us which was in Christ Jesus (Phil. 2:5).

So we must stand at the door of our mind—and choose. We keep out hate, revenge, resentment—any negatives, and bring in love—and life.

So choose joy and happiness. It is yours

The Spirit

The Spirit itself beareth witness with our spirit, that we are the children of God. (Rom. 8:16)

And if children, then heirs; heirs of God, and joint-heirs with Christ. (Rom. 8:17)

When our spirit connects with the Spirit of God within us, we become children of God and joint heirs with Christ.

And when we live with our body, mind, and spirit in God, we bear fruit—the fruit the tree bears when it comes to full maturity.

It takes patience, wisdom, and a special dedication on our part to make the "fruits of the Spirit" our response to life. It is the "mind of Christ" (I Cor. 2:16) which dwells within us that makes us the overcomers. We then have become integrated—whole. For then the Holy Spirit fills our heart with the love of God (Rom. 5:5).

And the fruits of the Spirit are love, joy, peace, long-suffering, gentleness, goodness, faith, meekness, and temperance (Gal. 5:22–23).

When we analyze each one of the "fruits" we find that we have all the qualities for a Christian life.

JOY affirms love's strength. "The joy of the LORD is your strength." (Neh. 8:10)

PEACE affirms love's security. "And the peace of God, which passeth all understanding, shall keep your hearts and minds through Christ Jesus." (Phil. 4:7)

LONG-SUFFERING affirms love's patience. "In your patience possess ye your souls." (Luke 21:19)

198

GENTLENESS affirms love's conduct. "Thy gentleness hath made me great." (Ps. 18:35)

GOODNESS affirms love's character. "Surely goodness and mercy shall follow me all the days of my life." (Ps. 23:6)

FAITH affirms love's confidence. "The LORD shall be thy confidence." (Prov. 3:26)

MEEKNESS affirms love's humility. "Before honor is humility." (Prov. 15:33)

TEMPERANCE affirms love's victory. "For whatsoever is born of God overcometh the world: and this is the victory that overcometh the world, even, our faith." (I John 5:4)

The Full and Balanced Life

The works of the LORD are great. . . . He hath made his wonderful works to be remembered. (Ps. 111:2, 4)

There is a secret to staying young in body, mind, and spirit. This special quality leads to the full and balanced life—mentally, physically, and spiritually. It is having a deep curiosity about life with a continual sense of wonder—a child's awe—about life and the universe.

I have seen young people who didn't have this special quality about loving life who were old before their time. And I have seen older people with a sense of learning, of wondering, and loving life who were eternally young.

My friend Martha is a person who has this special love of life. Although she is now past seventy, she still has an insatiable love for and curiosity about life.

Martha lives in the little house on the corner alone, but never lonely. For her house is always full of love and activity. Every corner reflects her interest in life and her love of God—and people. There are books, records, plants, and various collections of the curious and different that she has gathered from all over.

First when you enter her home you notice Martha's love for the Bible. She collects Bible translations and has a wall covered with them along with commentaries and other books on the Bible. For years Martha has taught Bible classes and has also written about the joys of living a Christian life. For she believes that Christians should not be long-faced or dour, but happy and joyful. "It's just as easy to be joyful and keep your mind filled with the joy of the Lord," she says. "Besides, joy multiplies!"

On another wall we find biographies of favorite people—the "overcomers" of life—those who showed what living the Christ way could do. To name just a few we see books by Madame Guyon, St. John of the Cross, John Calvin, the Wesley brothers, Norman Grubb, and Henrietta Mears.

Next we come to the kitchen, colorful and bright, filled with hanging plants and shelves of canned fruits, vegetables, preserves and jellies, giving the kitchen a stained-glass look. She shows us golden jars of jelly made from the yellow fruit of the exotic loquat tree that was plentiful this year.

There are books on nutrition, cooking, and gardening. Martha is well known for her herb and vegetable gardens as well as her fruit trees.

At lunch she usually serves a seven-sprout salad, made of nutritious sprouts she grows herself. And dessert time brings a piece of her mouth-watering banana-nut cream cake laden with calories "just this once."

Then we come to the travel and adventure section of Martha's house. Although she can't travel any longer because of physical problems, she now travels vicariously with everyone from T. E. Lawrence to Thor Heyerdahl of Kon-Tiki fame to traveling the seas with Jacques Cousteau.

And this frail ninety-five-pound woman has a special bond with Mount Everest, the tallest mountain in the world. She has a huge map of the mountain pinned to the wall and follows Edmund Hillary and those who came after him who conquer the mountain.

Then we come to the music section of her home. Her collections of records and music could keep one busy for days. Her taste is eclectic—everything from folk songs to jazz to gospel. At her bell collection she plays us "Open My Eyes That I May See" on her handbells. She says this is her favorite hymn and in a way is her "theme song."

This is just the "tip of the iceberg" of Martha's love of life. For all of God's universe is beautiful to her and she expresses it daily. By the way, her current project is saving up for a telescope so she can more clearly watch Halley's comet when it returns in 1985!

And when I asked Martha what her favorite Scripture was, she thought a moment and said it is a different one every day, according to the occasion. Today it was this one:

"For ye shall go out with joy, and be led forth with peace: the mountains and the hills shall break forth before you into singing, and all the trees of the field shall clap their hands." (Isa. 55:12)

RESOURCES

The whole Christian woman—body, mind, and spirit—is made whole through Christ. And we give thanks for our resources that keep us living joyfully and productively in the Kingdom.

FOR WE KNOW

Therefore if any man be in Christ, he is a new creature: old things are passed away; behold, all things are become new. (II Cor. 5:17)

AND

As many as touched him were made perfectly whole. (Matt. 14:36)

AND WE ARE TOLD ABOUT OUR BODY

Know ye not that ye are the temple of God, and that the Spirit of God dwelleth in you? (I Cor. 3:16)

The light of the body is the eye: therefore when thine eye is single, thy whole body also is full of light. (Luke 11:34)

SO

Present your bodies a living sacrifice, holy, acceptable unto God. (Rom. 12:1)

AND OUR MIND IS IMPORTANT, FOR

As he thinketh in his heart, so is he. (Prov. 23:7)

BUT WE HAVE THIS PROMISE

Thou wilt keep him in perfect peace, whose mind is stayed on thee. (Isa. 26:3)

AND WE ARE TOLD

Let this mind be in you, which was also in Christ Jesus. (Phil. 2:5)

For God hath not given us the spirit of fear; but of power, and of love, and of a sound mind. (II Tim. 1:7)

AND WE KNOW
The peace of God, which passeth all understanding, shall keep your hearts and minds through Christ Jesus. (Phil. 4:7)

AND OUR SPIRIT IS OUR LINK WITH GOD
For as many as are led by the Spirit of God, they are the sons of God. (Rom. 8:14)

FOR
The Spirit itself beareth witness with our spirit, that we are the children of God. (Rom. 8:16)

And if children, then heirs; heirs of God, and joint-heirs with Christ. (Rom. 8:17)

WHICH MAKES US
Rejoice with joy unspeakable and full of glory. (I Peter 1:8)

FOR WE KNOW
We are all the children of God by faith in Christ Jesus. (Gal. 3:26)

AND WE ALSO HAVE THIS PROMISE
Well done, thou good and faithful servant: . . . enter thou into the joy of thy Lord. (Matt. 25:21)

FOR HE SAYS TO US
O woman, great is thy faith. (Matt. 15:28)

Yea, I have loved thee with an everlasting love. (Jer. 31:3)